Advanced BASIC2
Programs for the
Amstrad PC

Advanced BASIC2 Programs for the Amstrad PC

P.K. McBride

HEINEMANN
NEW·TECH

William Heinemann Ltd
10 Upper Grosvenor Street, London W1X 9PA

LONDON   MELBOURNE   AUCKLAND

First published 1988
©*P.K. McBride 1988*

British Library Cataloguing in Publication Data
McBride, P.K.
Advanced BASIC2 Programs on the Amstrad PC
1. Amstrad PC microcomputer systems.
Programming languages. Basic language
I. Title
005.2'65
ISBN 0-434-91280-8

Typeset by
Colin Powell Typesetting, Bournemouth, Dorset
Printed and bound in Great Britain by
Dotesios, Bradford on Avon, Wiltshire

CONTENTS

CONTENTS

PART 3: Graphics and screen displays

PART 4: Random-access files

INTRODUCTION

BASIC2 PROGRAMMING

Basic2 is a very satisfying language to work with − it's not perfect, but then, no programming language ever is. There are a few things that could have been implemented better, and some regrettable omissions, but these are more that outweighed by Basic2's many attractive features. It's fast and friendly; the string- and number-handling facilities are very good; there are comprehensive filing and disk-access functions; and it does give you a superb control of the screen.

That line numbers are optional seems a little strange at first, but after a little while you realise what an unnecessary encumbrance they are. I never use them. Subroutines are much easier to handle by label names than by line numbers, and GOTO plays a very limited role in Basic2 programming. With FOR..NEXT, REPEAT..UNTIL and WHILE..WEND all available, you do not need to use GOTO to loop back to repeat a set of lines; and a well-ordered structure of subroutines is much easier to write and quicker to debug than a long straggle of lines held together by a spaghetti tangle of GOTO jumps.

But no doubt I am preaching to the converted. This book is about advanced Basic2 programming and I am assuming that you already use, and enjoy using, that language. There's no attempt here to explain in detail how individual commands and functions should be used, except in those areas which may present problems to the less experienced user. A brief summary of Basic2 command and functions is included as an appendix, mainly for convenience. The Amstrad PCs have fairly large footprints and by the time you have spread a few sheets of notes on the desk as well, there may not be room for a reference manual as well as this book!

The programs have been grouped into four parts: text and number handling, sequential files, graphics and finally random-access files. In practice there is a very considerable degree of overlap − file handling, for example, is an essential part of most programs, and you will find some hefty calculations where images are being transformed in two or three dimensions. The 'self-taught computer' could perhaps have been put in a section headed 'Artificial Intelligence', but that seemed too grand a title for a program that merely allows the computer to teach itself how to play noughts and crosses.

Within each group, and overall, there is a progression of complexity. Each individual program is fully documented, so that they can be tackled in any order, but you may sometimes need to refer back to earlier chapters for explanations of particular techniques or concepts. The choice and design of the programs have been governed by educational considerations as much as by practical ones. I wanted to produce a set that would not only demonstrate a range of techniques, but that could also be put to good use − either directly or after some adaptation to suit your own needs.

Each program focuses on a different aspect of Basic2 programming and the flip side of this approach is that unnecessary details and refinements are avoided. There is only limited error-trapping; screen displays are kept deliberately simple − except in those programs that explore screen-handling; and there is a notable absence of Help screens. All of these would have increased the length and apparent complexity of the programs, without actually making them any more effective. They can be added quite simply if you want to give your programs a professional gloss, but by leaving them out of these listings we have been able to concentrate on the things that matter.

You will find that the each program has been written as a series of distinct subroutines. This makes it much easier to explain how the programs work and, in addition, should make it easier for you to adapt them or take routines from different programs and use them in new applications of your own. But, convenience apart, this is the way that Basic2 programs must be written if you want to avoid an untidy mess of GOTOs and LABELs.

To make the programs easier to read, label and variable names are all more or less self-explanatory. This does mean that they tend to be on the long side and you may wish to abbreviate them when typing in the programs.

PART 1

TEXT AND NUMBERS

Chapter 1

Random Number Generator

The purpose of this program is to generate sets of random numbers for use in simulations or as samples for testing statistical techniques. Outputs from here might be used, for example, in checking the analysis and display routines of the STATS program that is described in the next chapter.

The program is simple, but flexible. The user can specify the bottom and top limits of the range of random numbers, how many to include in the set and whether they are to have an equal or a Normal distribution. The sets can be output either to the screen, a printer or to disk.

An equal distribution is one in which there will be an even spread of numbers across the whole range. If you roll a die, for example, each number has an equal chance of coming up. A Normal distribution, on the other hand, is one where the numbers cluster around a central value. As any Monopoly player knows, roll two dice and you are more likely to get a total of 7 than any other value:

1 + 6, 2 + 5, 3 + 4, 4 + 3, 5 + 2 and 6 + 1

All add up to 7, but only double sixes give you 12. Normal distributions crop up all around us in the real world — the more obvious examples include people's height and weight, examination marks, the accuracy with which assembly-line machines fill packets or manufacture components. All of these will tend to cluster around an average, with very few extreme values.

Program structure

Main loop

> Repeat
> > Get range, number and type of randoms
> > Get output choice
> > On choice..
> > > Disk − get filename then print
> > > Screen − print, then hold screen until ready
> > > Printer − check ready then print
> > Offer another set
> Until no more sets wanted

Key subroutines

> Print random number (equal or normal) to selected stream

> Press any key when ready

Notes

Output streams

Output from Basic2 can be to any of the four screen windows, the printer, a disk file or an RS232 link, if present. The data is sent to its destination via a *stream*, with Streams #1 to #4 normally taking output to Windows #1 to #4, Stream #0 leading to the printer, and Streams #5 and upwards being reserved for disk files. Note the use of the word 'normally'. These are the default values, but you can link any stream to any output device.

Unless you specify to the contrary, all output is directed via the default stream to the current screen window. In this particular example, the current window is #1 (headed 'Results 1'), and data travels via Stream #1. To switch output to any other device, we can either change the default stream by the command 'STREAM #number', or − more flexibly − include the stream number within the PRINT statement.

You will notice in the program that the selection of output leads to the subroutines *diskout*, *screenout* and *printout*. In each of these, the variable *where* is set to the appropriate stream number. Then, in the routine *outrand*, random numbers are output via the line:

```
PRINT #where.x,
```

This same method of redirecting to different streams is used in all subsequent programs where there is a choice of output device.

Disk files

Before data can be sent to a disk file, a stream must be explicitly opened by the command:

```
OPEN #streamnumber OUTPUT filename
```

The selected stream can be any one that is not currently in use. Here it could have been Stream #2, as Window #2 is not needed by the program. Using Streams #5 and upwards does have the advantage that the four default window streams are left untouched should they be needed in later developments of the program. The stream number can be given as variables, or as a number, and the filename can be a string variable or in "text" form.

The names given to disk files must be no more than eight characters long and may include a three-character extension after the name. Upper- or lower-case letters can be used when specifying the names. The first half of the *diskout* routine forces the filename into the standard format.

```
WHILE LEN(file$)<8:file$=file$+" ":WEND
IF LEN(file$)>8 THEN file$=LEFT$(file$,8)
file$=UPPER$(file$)+".RND"
```

These lines pad out the filename with spaces if it is shorter than eight characters, crop it to length if it is too long and, finally, convert it to upper case before adding the extension .RND. The purpose of this is to make it easier for you to identify the random number files when searching through the disk directory. Any three-character extension can be used and it can be omitted if you prefer.

In practice, much of this routine is unnecessary. When the filename is written into the disk directory the MS-DOS system will automatically convert it to upper case and bring it up to the standard eight-character length. The only thing that must be done to avoid an 'Invalid filename' error, is to crop an over-long name. So why bother with the rest? As much as anything else, it is a matter of establishing good habits. In other programs, where files are being specified for reading back in, the filename needs to be in the right format so that it can be checked against the files found on the disk. The filename formatting routine that is used here will be re-used again in all subsequent programs that access files.

When you have finished with a disk file the stream must be closed, before leaving the program, with the command:

```
CLOSE #streamnumber
```

Failure to do so will have two ill effects. Disk files are buffered, i.e. data sent to them is held initially in a reserved area of memory. When that memory space is full, or when the stream is closed, the data is written to the disk. If you quit the program without closing the stream, data may be lost. Secondly, any attempt to re-open a stream that has not been closed will produce a 'Stream in use' error message.

Equal and Normal distributions of random numbers

The Basic2 random number function in the form 'RND(n)' will produce a random integer in the range 1 to n. It will be an equal distribution, in that every number in the range will have the same chance of cropping up. Thus RND(6) simulates a die. To produce a random number in a range that starts at anything other than 1, add in a displacement value. RND(10) + 10 would give you a number between 11 and 20.

In this program, the limits of the random numbers are held in the variables *low* and *high*. If the bottom limit is to be included in the set − and the program assumes that it is to be − then the *low* value must be pushed down one: *low = low − 1*. The *range* can be calculated from these by: *high − low*. So, when an equal distribution random number is wanted, the expression is:

```
x=RND(range)+low
```

For example, given an input *low* value of 40 and a *high* of 60, *low* would be adjusted to 39, *range* would be 21 and the final formula, RND(21) + 39, would give numbers between 40 (1 + 39) and 60 (21 + 39).

The 'two-dice' approach is the simplest method of simulating a Normal distribution, and it should be sufficiently accurate for most purposes. To work out the operations needed for this, look at what happens in reality; two dice (range 1 to 6) will give numbers between 2 and 12. We need to get the expression RND(6) + RND(6) out of the input values *low = 2* and *high = 12*. It is achieved in the lines:

```
IF dist$="N" THEN low= low-2:range=(high-low)/2

-  ..... x=RND(range)+RND(range)+low
```

So, if you wanted numbers between 80 and 120, clustering around the mid-point, these calculations give a *low* of 78 and a *range* of 21 = (120 − 78)/2. The lowest possible number will be 80 (1 + 1 + 78) and the highest 120 (21 + 21 + 78). The most common number will be 100 which can be produced in 21 different ways:

1 + 21 + 78, 2 + 20 + 78, 3 + 19 + 78, ...

and so on.

Random number generator program

```
REM random number generator

SCREEN #1 TEXT 80 FIXED,22 FIXED
WINDOW #1 FULL ON

LABEL mainloop
REPEAT
  CLS
  PRINT "Range of numbers?"
  INPUT "Lowest ";low
  INPUT "Highest ";high
  INPUT "How many random numbers ?",number
  INPUT "Equal or Normal distribution? (E/N) ",dist$
  dist$=UPPER$(dist$)
  IF dist$="E" THEN low=low-1:range=high-low
  IF dist$="N" THEN low=low-2:range=(high-low)/2
  INPUT "Output to Screen, Printer or Disk ? (S/P/D)",out$
  out$=UPPER$(out$)

  IF out$="S" THEN GOSUB screenout
  IF out$="P" THEN GOSUB printout
  IF out$="D" THEN GOSUB diskout

  PRINT "Another set? (Y/N)"
  again$=""
  REPEAT
    again$=UPPER$(INKEY$)
  UNTIL again$="Y" OR again$="N"
UNTIL again$="N"

END

LABEL diskout
DRIVE "B":REM please yourself which drive

INPUT "Filename for this set?";file$
WHILE LEN(file$)<8:file$=file$+" ":WEND
IF LEN(file$)>8 THEN file$=LEFT$(file$,8)
file$=UPPER$(file$)+".RND"
 REM formatting filename not essential, but useful
where=5
 REM any stream can be used for disk filing
OPEN #5 OUTPUT file$
GOSUB outrand
```

```
CLOSE 5
RETURN

LABEL screenout
where=1
GOSUB outrand
GOSUB anykey
RETURN

LABEL printout
PRINT "Check that printer is ready"
GOSUB anykey
where=0
GOSUB outrand
RETURN

LABEL outrand
FOR loop=1 TO number
  IF dist$="E" THEN x=RND(range)+low ELSE x=RND(range)+RND(range)+low
  PRINT #where,x,
NEXT loop
PRINT #where
RETURN

LABEL anykey
PRINT "Press any key to go on."
ky$=""
REPEAT
  ky$=INKEY$
UNTIL ky$<>""
RETURN
```

Chapter 2

Statistical Analysis and Graphs

This program will take in data — either in raw form or grouped into classes or under headings — perform some numerical analysis and display the figures as bar charts, line graphs, ogives or pie charts. It can handle up to five sets of figures simultaneously, so that comparisons can be made between related sets, and these may contain up to 100 individual items or 20 groups. A few definitions may be useful.

Raw data consists of figures as they are first collected, before any ordering, sorting or grouping has been done. For example, the examination marks of two classes of students might be gathered as follows:

Class A

25	71	56	84	53	40	62	74	46	52	29	51
64	32	67	43	14	65	57	69	57	36	55	59

Class B

36	61	75	41	68	52	45	57	33	81	53	43
50	84	39	66	24	76	44	58	70	49		

Where data is to be given this way the program will first ask for the number of sets of figures, then take in the items in each set. The sets do not have to be the same size and you do not need to specify at the outset how many numbers are in a set. Just keep typing them in until you are done, then enter *999* to end. (If 999 could be a valid figure in your sets, then a different number will have to be used as an end-marker.)

Once the raw data has been entered the program will group it into classes using whatever boundaries you choose. In this example, class intervals of 10 would seem reasonable, so the boundaries will be 0, 10, 20, 30 and so on. After processing, the data will be in the form shown in Table 2.1.

TABLE 2.1

	1-10	11-20	21-30	31-40	41-50	51-60	61-70	71-80	81-90	91-100
Class A	0	1	2	2	4	7	5	2	1	0
Class B	0	0	1	3	5	5	3	3	2	0

Grouped data can consist of either *discrete* or *continuous* variables. Discrete variables are those where the data falls naturally into distinct classes — types of vehicles in a traffic survey, sales of different lines of goods, or profit and loss figures on a monthly basis. The classes will be labelled with short text headings — 'Cars', 'Trucks', 'Buses', 'Cycles', etc.

With continuous variables, there are no such natural breaks and a class structure must be imposed upon the data by setting boundaries, as with the examination results above. Here the boundary figures will be used as the headings, e.g. 1−10, 11−20, 21−30, and so on.

The numerical analysis section will calculate the *mean* and *standard deviation* of each set of numbers. Exactly how the standard deviation, that much-used measure of spread, is calculated will be covered later in the notes to the program. For the moment it is enough to say that the standard deviation is a number such that two-thirds of all the values in a set will fall between one standard deviation either side of the mean.

The numerical analysis and any of the graphing options may be omitted if you do not need them. Apart from cutting out the labelled routines, all you will need to do is to remove them from the menu at the start and adjust the ON...GOSUB.. line that controls the flow of the program.

Program structure

Initialisation

Arrays — raw and grouped data, boundaries, mid-points, headings
Graphics screen

Main loop

R e p e a t	
Display menu and get option	*begin*
Perform option	
Grouped data	*grouped*
Data from disk	
Data from keyboard	*newdata*
get boundaries	*getgroups*
get headings	*getheads*
Raw data entry and grouping	*raw*
Numerical analysis	*analyse*
Draw bar chart	*bar*
Draw line graph	*linegraph*
Draw ogive	*ogives*
Draw pie chart	*piechart*
Until exit selected	*exit*

Key subroutines

Save new data to disk	*savegroup*
Format filename	*filenames*
Scale figures before graphing	*scaling*
Press any key to continue	*anykey*

Notes

Arrays

The program as written can only cope with a maximum of five sets, with 20 classes or 100 raw values to a set. These could be increased, though there are certain practical limits. With the grouped data you will run into display problems if there are too many classes. Even five sets of 20 classes gives you 100 separate bars on the bar charts — far too many for a meaningful graph. There is no reason why you should not have more than 100 items in the raw data arrays, but it will involve a lot of keying in!

As memory space is not a problem with this program in its current form, no attempt has been made to be economical with the array definitions. Should you wish to expand the program or the arrays substantially, then space can be saved here.

The program treats all arrays as if their first subscript was 1, whereas arrays are in fact numbered from 0 unless you specify otherwise. The following expression would cut down the memory used by the *raw* array from roughly 3K to about 2.5K:

```
DIM raw(1 to 5,1 to 100)
```

If the values in the arrays are all integers, then an appropriate integer format can be specified for them, saving considerable amounts of space. The main alternatives are:

Type	Value range	Bytes/element
BYTE	-128 to +127	1
UBYTE	0 to 255	1
WORD	-32768 to +32767	2
UWORD	0 to 65535	2

You can also define numbers as INTEGER, which will cope with whole numbers from approximately -2 billion to $+2$ billion, but as this takes 4 bytes/element, there is little saving over the real number type.

So, if you knew in advance that the raw data would only consist of whole positive numbers, never higher than 65000, use the command:

```
DIM raw(1 to 5,1 to 100) UWORD
```

This array will take up only around 1K of memory.

Re-dimensioned arrays

Another way of using memory more efficiently is to dimension the arrays to the exact size required for the sets of data. Instead of setting up standard arrays at the start of the program, you would include the following line within the data entry routine:

```
DIM group(sets,groupnum)
```

If you use this method, then note that the DIM command can not be used on an array that has already been dimensioned. You must remove the old array first by using **CLEAR**. Take care with this as it erases ALL variables! It should be written at the start of the *newdata* routine as there are no active variables at that point.

Graphics screen

As this is predominantly a graphics program, I have opted to use a graphics screen at all times. Since the use of windows is not a prime concern here, only a single one is opened. It might be more efficient to define Screen #1 as Text for the menu, the data entry and the analysis routines, and redefine it as Graphics for the charts. Text screens can be manipulated faster by Basic2, though speed is not a problem here. Hence a simple, single definition at the start.

The USER SPACE is set to 640 by 200, rather than left at the default values of 5000 each way. Where output is only to the screen, it makes sense to keep the co-ordinates at pixel size. Using the default values will not improve the resolution and the smaller numbers are easier to handle. Users of the 1640 may wish to alter this to 640 by 350. If this is done, the y values in the *scaling* and *piechart* routines should be multiplied by 1.75 to bring them up to scale.

Grouped data entry

The first stage here is to get the number of groups and either the boundaries or the headings. You will see that when the boundaries are set, in the *getgroups* routine, it is done by taking the lower limit of each group, then a final value for the top limit of the highest group. Once the boundaries are known, they are converted into headings, for the graphs, by the line:

```
head$(gn)=STR$(bound(gn))+"-"+STR$(bound(gn+1))
```

Mid-points are found within the same loop by adding together the two adjacent boundary values and dividing by 2.

The data entry screen is laid out in tabular form, with set numbers across the top and group headings down the left-hand side. The frequencies for the groups are then keyed in, one set at a time. As they are entered, they are added up to find the total frequencies for each set (*itemcount*).

The lowest and highest data values are found during data entry and stored in *mini* and *maxi*. They are needed later in calculating the vertical scale for the graphic displays.

The value of *mini* is initially set to 999, then revalued − if necessary − within the data entry loop by the line:

```
IF group(sn,gn) < mini THEN mini=group(sn,gn)
```

where *sn* is the set number and *gn* the group number. An equivalent line will raise *maxi* from its start point of −999 to the highest value in the set.

Raw data entry

At the start of this routine the user is asked for the number of items in the sets, *rawnum*. This value is then used as the limit for the collecting loop, though an 'early exit' is offered through the use of the rogue value '999'. This may need to be altered if 999 is a possible data item.

Once the raw data has been collected, it is converted into grouped form. Group boundaries are found, using the *getgroups* routine, then each individual raw data value is compared with the group boundaries and added into the appropriate group. It is a process equivalent to the use of a tally count when working out frequency distributions manually. The key line here is:

```
IF raw(sn,rn) > bound(gn) AND raw(sn,rn) <= bound(gn+1) ....
- THEN group(sn,gn)=group(sn,gn)+1
```

Note the way that the greater than and lesser than signs are used here. It means that, given the boundaries 0, 10 and 20, the group ranges are actually 0.01 to 10 and 10.01 to 20 (taken to two decimal places). Thus, the value 10 would be added into the first group, not the second. It also means that a raw data value of 0 would not fit into either group. If you want to arrange the program so that these same boundaries would give group ranges of 0 to 9.99 and 10 to 19.99, then start that line with the test:

```
IF raw(sn,rn) >= bound(gn) AND raw(sn,rn) < bound(gn)....
```

As the program stands, there is no facility to amend either grouped or raw data once it has been entered, but this could be added very readily if it was needed. The transformation programs and all the file-handling programs have routines for editing stored data that could be adapted to suit this.

Disk files

Data is stored on the disk in this order:

setnum	number of sets
groupnum	number of groups
mini	minimum items in a group
maxi	maximum items in a group
vartype	type of data (1 = continuous, 2 = discrete)

For every group
head$()	heading
bound()	boundaries − continuous data only

For every set
group()	data
bound(gn+1)	top boundary
itemcount()	total in each set

22

Disk space and disk access time can both be trimmed if only the *head$* array was saved and not the boundaries. When the file is loaded back in, these values could be found from within the headings by string slicing.

At present, sets are identified by number only. If you wish to add labels for the sets, then these could be stored with the *itemcount* in the final loop.

If you intend to adapt the program so that data can be edited after entry, then you should also add a routine to save raw data in its original form, rather than after it has been processed. A 'Load data from disk' option can then be spliced into the raw data entry routine.

Numerical analysis

The *analyse* routine calculates mean and standard deviations. For discrete variables, the **Mean** is total number of items divided by the number of groups and is a simple calculation:

```
mean=itemcount(sn)/groupnum
```

Where data is of the continuous variable type, the total of the set is found by multiplying the frequency (the number in each group) by the mid-point and adding these values together. This result is then divided by the total number of items in the set:

```
FOR gn=1 TO groupnum
total=total+mid(gn)*group(sn,gn)
NEXT gn
mean=total/itemcount(sn)
```

The **Standard Deviation** calculations will only work with continuous variables. In practice this is not a significant problem as the measure is of limited value with discrete data. The standard deviation is calculated in several stages:

1   Find the mean of the set.

2   Find the *deviation* − the difference between the mid-point and the mean for each group.

3   Square the deviations, multiply them by the number in each group and add them together.

4   Find the mean squared deviation, by dividing the total by the number of items in the set.

5   Take the square root to get the standard deviation.

This translates into the routine:

```
FOR gn=1 TO groupnum
dev=mid(gn)-mean
stotal=stotal+dev^2*group(sn,gn)
NEXT gn
smean=stotal/itemcount(sn)
sdev=SQR(mean)
```

A worked example of a mean and standard deviation calculation is shown in Table 2.2 for comparison.

TABLE 2.2

Mid-points	Frequency	M-P*F	QSDeviation	Deviation^2*S
10	3	30	-40	4800
30	6	180	-20	2400
50	12	600	0	0
70	6	420	20	2400
90	3	270	40	4800
	TOTAL	1500	STOTAL	14400
	MEAN	50	SMEAN	480
			SDEV	21.9

The main value of the standard deviation is in giving a measure of spread. The calculation is such that two-thirds of all the items in a set will fall within 1 S.D. above or below the mean, and virtually all of the items will fall between 3 S.D. either way. It is a far better way of describing a set than simply using the mean by itself.

Suppose, for example, that you had two machines that were supposed to fill packets with 1000 g of Whizzo. Packets filled by machine A have a mean weight of 1000 g; those filled by machine B have a mean weight of 1002 g. Machine A would therefore seem to be the better machine. Further calculation then shows that the 'A' packets have an S.D. of 10, while the 'B' set have an S.D. of only 2. This tells us that those filled by machine B will rarely contain more than 8 g overweight, while machine A will pour 30 g or more extra Whizzo into its packets. Machine B is therefore the most economical machine to use.

Scaling

As the program is intended for general use, the number of items in any given group could range from one to many thousands. The y values must therefore be scaled to make best use of the screen height. Similarly, as there could be anything up to 100 items to display (5*20 groups), x values must also be scaled. The *scaling* routine opens:

```
scope=maxi-mini
marks=scope/10
yscale=160/scope      (change to 280/scope on a 1640)
xmark=540/groupnum
xscale=xmark/setnum
```

If the vertical scales on the graphs are always to start at 0, then *scope = maxi* and *mini* serves no purpose.

The *marks* value fixes the divisions on the vertical scale. As it stands, these will only have nice round numbers when *scope* is easily divisible. You may wish to add a series of lines that would round *marks* up to the nearest digit, 10, 100 or whatever. If you do so, then test the displays afterwards across a whole range of *scope* values to make sure that it can cope with awkward numbers.

The *xscale* variable is only needed for bar charts, where the data for each set will form a separate bar within the space allocated by *xmark* to each group.

The central part of the *scaling* routine draws the axes for the graphs, and 1640 users will need to multiply the y values here by 1.75 if they have set the USER SPACE to 640 by 350.

The final few lines display a key — the colour of each bar or lines is *1 + set number*. A series of coloured blocks and set numbers will be drawn down from the top right of the screen by the loop:

```
FOR sn=1 to setnum
BOX 560;200-sn*10, 24, 8 COLOUR 1+sn FILL WITH 8
MOVE 590;200-sn*10: PRINT sn
NEXT sn
```

Bar charts

The routine starts by calling the *scaling* subroutine. The *xwidth* is then set to 90% of the *xscale* value so that there is clear space between the bars.

The bars are produced by the BOX command, and as the bottom y value and the x width are fixed, only the left-hand x value and the height need further calculation. This is done and the bars are drawn by a pair of nested loops; but note the way that these start at 0, rather than 1. This ensures that the first bar will start close to the vertical axis. Notice also that the routine checks for zero values before attempting to draw a bar:

```
FOR gn=0 TO groupnum-1
   FOR sn=0 TO setnum-1
   x=30+xmark*gn+xscale*sn
   y=(group(sn+1,gn+1)-mini)*yscale
   IF y>0 THEN BOX x;32,xwidth,y COLOUR 2+sn FILL
NEXT sn
NEXT gn
```

Ogives

These are also called cumulative frequency curves and in two separate lines they show the total items above or below each of the class boundaries. If they were being drawn manually, you would first need to work out the cumulative totals, as is shown in Table 2.3 using the examination results from Class A above.

As these are cumulative frequency displays, the *maxi* value must be raised to highest *itemcount* figure, before the *scaling* routine is called.

The 'Total Below' line is drawn first. Each *group* value is added in turn to the *total* to find the next y co-ordinate for plotting. Once that is finished, the 'Total Above' line is produced by successively reducing the *total*.

Pie charts

Perhaps the most obscure part of this routine is the first section which sets up alternative layouts for 1, 2, 3, 4 or 5 pie diagrams. There are six lines of DATA. The last five of these hold the radius and the x,y co-ordinates of the centres of the pies. The first line determines how far to go through these data items before starting to pick up the ones that are relevant to the situation:

```
FOR sn=1 TO setnum:READ howfar:NEXT sn
FOR n=1 TO howfar:READ dummy:NEXT n
DATA 4,6,10,16,24
DATA 180,340,100
DATA 140,200,100,490,100
DATA 110,320,135,120,70,510,70
DATA 100,200,150,440,150,120,50,520,50
DATA 90,140,150,500,150,320,100,140,50,500,50
READ radius
FOR sn=1 TO setnum
READ x,y
```

TABLE 2.3

	1-10	11-20	21-30	31-40	41-50	51-60	61-70	71-80	81-90	91-100
Class A	0	1	2	2	4	7	5	2	1	0
Total Below	10	20	30	40	50	60	70	80	90	100
	0	1	3	5	9	16	21	23	24	24
Total Above	0	10	20	30	40	50	60	70	80	90
	24	24	23	21	19	15	8	3	1	0

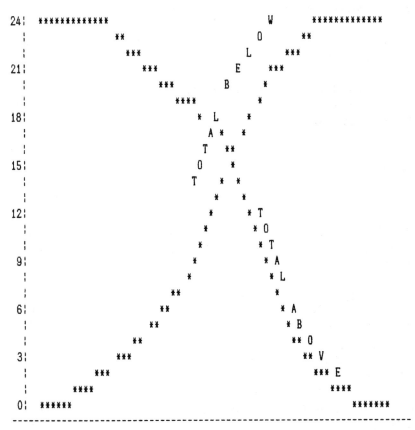

For example, if there were three sets of variables to be charted, *howfar* would take the value 10. The second loop would then READ 10 items into *dummy*, so that the data pointer stood at the start of the fourth line of DATA. The *radius* is then READ in as 110, and the first *x,y* co-ordinates as 320 and 135.

Each pie segment is drawn by the lines:

```
arcsize=group(sn,gn)/itemcount(gn)
arcend=arcstart+arcsize
ELLIPTICAL PIE x;y,radius,0.5,arcstart,arcend COLOUR gn FILL WITH 8
arcstart=arcend
```

Here, *arcsize* converts the *group* value to a fraction of the set's total, expressed in degrees.

Where the USER SPACE has been set to 640 by 350, the y co-ordinates of the pie centres will need adjustment. So will the distortion factor (currently set to 0.5), if the pies are to remain circular.

Statistics program

```
REM statistics

DIM raw(5,100),group(5,20),bound(21),mid(20),head$(20)
REM raw()=raw data;group()=grouped data;bound()=boundaries;mid()=mid-points
REM rawnum=no.of raw data items;groupnum=no. of groups
file$="None"
OPTION DEGREES

LABEL begin
SCREEN #1 GRAPHICS 640 FIXED,200 FIXED
USER SPACE 640,200
REPEAT
  WINDOW TITLE "Current File "+file$
  WINDOW FULL ON
  CLS

  PRINT AT (24;2);"DATA ENTRY"
  PRINT AT (25;4);"Grouped Data...............1"
  PRINT AT (25;6);"Raw Data...................2"
  PRINT AT (25;8);"Numerical Analysis.........3"
  PRINT AT (25;10);"GRAPHS"
```

```
PRINT AT (25;12);"Bar Chart.................4"
PRINT AT (25;14);"Line Graph................5"
PRINT AT (25;16);"Ogives....................6"
PRINT AT (25;18);"Pie Chart.................7"
PRINT AT (25;20);"Exit......................8"

 opt$=""
 WHILE opt$<"1" OR opt$>"8"
   opt$=INKEY$
 WEND
 opt=VAL(opt$)
 ON opt GOSUB grouped,raw,analyse,bar,linegraph,ogives,piechart,exit
UNTIL opt=8
END


LABEL grouped
CLS
INPUT "New Data or Load from disk (N/L) ";a$
IF UPPER$(a$)="N" THEN GOTO newdata
GOSUB filenames
IF x$<>file$ THEN PRINT "File Not Found":GOSUB anykey:GOTO grouped
OPEN #5 INPUT file$
INPUT #5,setnum,groupnum,mini,maxi,vartype
FOR gn=1 TO groupnum
  IF vartype=1 THEN INPUT #5,bound(gn)
  INPUT #5,head$(gn)
  FOR sn=1 TO setnum
    INPUT #5,group(sn,gn)
  NEXT sn
NEXT gn
IF vartype=1 THEN INPUT #5,bound(groupnum+1):GOSUB head_mid
FOR sn=1 TO setnum
  INPUT #5,itemcount(sn)
NEXT sn
CLOSE #5
RETURN


LABEL newdata
INPUT "Discrete or Continuous Variables (D/C) ";a$
IF UPPER$(a$)="D" THEN vartype=2 ELSE vartype=1
IF vartype=1 THEN GOSUB getgroups ELSE GOSUB getheads

INPUT "Number of sets of variables (Max.5)";setnum
CLS
mini=999:maxi=-999
FOR gn=1 TO groupnum
```

```
    PRINT AT (1;gn+1);head$(gn)
NEXT gn
FOR sn=1 TO setnum
  itemcount(sn)=0
  FOR gn=1 TO groupnum
    PRINT AT (sn*12;1);"Set ";sn
    INPUT AT (sn*12;gn+1);group(sn,gn)
    itemcount(sn)=itemcount(sn)+group(sn,gn)
    IF group(sn,gn)<mini THEN mini=group(sn,gn)
    IF group(sn,gn)>maxi THEN maxi=group(sn,gn)
  NEXT gn
NEXT sn
GOSUB savegroup
RETURN


LABEL getgroups
INPUT "Number of groups (Max.20)";groupnum
FOR gn=1 TO groupnum
  PRINT "Lower boundary of group ";gn
  INPUT bound(gn)
NEXT gn
INPUT "Upper boundary of top group ";bound(groupnum+1)
vartype=1


LABEL head_mid
FOR gn=1 TO groupnum
  head$(gn)=STR$(bound(gn))+" - "+STR$(bound(gn+1))
  mid(gn)=(bound(gn)+bound(gn+1))/2
NEXT gn
RETURN


LABEL getheads
INPUT "Number of groups (Max.20)";groupnum
FOR gn=1 TO groupnum
  PRINT "Heading for group ";gn
  INPUT head$(gn)
NEXT gn
vartype=2
RETURN


LABEL raw
CLS
INPUT "Number of Sets of variables (Max. 5)";setnum
INPUT "Number of items of data per set (Max. 100)";rawnum
FOR sn=1 TO setnum
  PRINT "Set Number ";sn
```

30

```
    temp=rawnum
    FOR rn=1 TO rawnum
      INPUT "Data Item (999 to quit)";raw(sn,rn)
      IF raw(sn,rn)=999 THEN raw(sn,rn)=0:temp=rn:rn=rawnum

    LABEL nextnum
   NEXT rn
NEXT sn

PRINT "Converting to Grouped Form "

GOSUB getgroups
mini=999:maxi=-999
FOR sn=1 TO setnum
  FOR rn=1 TO rawnum
    FOR gn=1 TO groupnum
      IF raw(sn,rn)>bound(gn) AND raw(sn,rn)<=bound(gn+1)
    - THEN group(sn,gn)=group(sn,gn)+1
    NEXT gn
  NEXT rn
  itemcount(sn)=0
  FOR gn=1 TO groupnum
    itemcount(sn)=itemcount(sn)+group(sn,gn)
    IF mini>group(sn,gn) THEN mini=group(sn,gn)
    IF maxi<group(sn,gn) THEN maxi=group(sn,gn)
  NEXT gn
NEXT sn
GOSUB savegroup
RETURN

LABEL savegroup
INPUT "Save Data on disk (Y/N) ";a$
IF UPPER$(a$)="N" THEN RETURN
GOSUB filenames
a$="N"
WHILE x$=file$ AND a$="N"
  PRINT "File Already Exists"
  INPUT "Overwrite, New Name (O/N)";a$
  IF UPPER$(a$)="N" THEN GOSUB filenames
WEND

OPEN #5 OUTPUT file$
PRINT #5,setnum,groupnum,mini,maxi,vartype
FOR gn=1 TO groupnum
  IF vartype=1 THEN PRINT #5,bound(gn)
  PRINT #5,head$(gn)
```

```
    FOR sn=1 TO setnum
      PRINT #5,group(sn,gn)
    NEXT sn
  NEXT gn
  IF vartype=1 THEN PRINT #5,bound(groupnum+1)
  FOR sn=1 TO setnum
    PRINT #5,itemcount(sn)
  NEXT sn
  CLOSE #5
  GOSUB anykey
  RETURN

  LABEL filenames
  INPUT "Filename ";file$
  WHILE LEN(file$)<8:file$=file$+" ":WEND
  IF LEN(file$)>8 THEN file$=LEFT$(file$,8)
  file$=UPPER$(file$)+".DAT"
  x$=FIND$(file$)
  RETURN

  LABEL analyse
  CLS
  FOR sn=1 TO setnum
    total=0
     REM mean
    FOR gn=1 TO groupnum
      total=total+mid(gn)*group(sn,gn)
    NEXT gn
    IF vartype=1 THEN mean=total/itemcount(sn)
    IF vartype=2 THEN mean=itemcount(sn)/groupnum
    PRINT AT(1;sn*2)"Mean for set ";sn;" = ";mean

     REM standard deviation
    stotal=0
    FOR gn=1 TO groupnum
      dev=mid(gn)-mean
      stotal=stotal+dev^2*group(sn,gn)
    NEXT gn
    smean=stotal/itemcount(sn)
    sdev=SQR(smean)
    PRINT "Standard Deviation = ";sdev
  NEXT sn
  GOSUB anykey
  RETURN
```

```
LABEL bar
bar=1:GOSUB scaling
xwidth=xscale*.9
FOR gn=0 TO groupnum-1
  FOR sn=0 TO setnum-1
    x=30+xmark*gn+xscale*sn
    y=(group(sn+1,gn+1)-mini)*yscale
    IF y>0 THEN BOX x;32,xwidth,y COLOUR 2+sn FILL
  NEXT sn
NEXT gn
GOSUB anykey
RETURN

LABEL linegraph
bar=0:GOSUB scaling
FOR sn=1 TO setnum
  x1=30:y1=30+(group(sn,1)-mini)*yscale
  FOR gn=2 TO groupnum
    x2=30+xmark*(gn-1)
    y2=30+(group(sn,gn)-mini)*yscale
    LINE x1;y1,x2;y2 COLOUR 1+sn
    x1=x2:y1=y2
  NEXT gn
NEXT sn
GOSUB anykey
RETURN

LABEL ogives
maxtemp=maxi:maxi=0
mintemp=mini:mini=0
FOR sn=1 TO setnum
  IF itemcount(sn)>maxi THEN maxi=itemcount(sn)
NEXT sn
bar=0:GOSUB scaling
FOR sn=1 TO setnum
  x1=30:y1=30
  total=0
  FOR gn=1 TO groupnum
    x2=30+xmark*gn
    total=total+group(sn,gn)
    y2=total*yscale+30
    LINE x1;y1,x2;y2 COLOUR 1+sn
    x1=x2:y1=y2
  NEXT gn
  x1=30
  FOR gn=1 TO groupnum
```

```
      x2=30+xmark*gn
      total=total-group(sn,gn)
      y2=total*yscale+30
      LINE x1;y1,x2;y2 COLOUR 1+sn STYLE 2
      x1=x2:y1=y2
    NEXT gn
  NEXT sn
  maxi=maxtemp
  mini=mintemp
  GOSUB anykey
  RETURN

  LABEL scaling
  scope=maxi-mini
  marks=scope/10
  yscale=160/scope
  xmark=540/groupnum
  xscale=xmark/setnum
  CLS
  LINE 630;30,30;30,30;190
  FOR marknum=0 TO 10
    y=16*marknum+30
    LINE 30;y,25;y
    MOVE 0;y:PRINT POINTS(8);mini+marks*marknum
  NEXT marknum
  FOR gn=0 TO groupnum-1
    x=30+xmark*gn
    LINE x;30,x;20
    MOVE x;20:PRINT head$(gn+1)
    FOR sn=0 TO setnum-1
      x1=x+xscale*sn
      IF bar=1 THEN LINE x1;30,x1;25
    NEXT sn
  NEXT gn
  FOR sn=1 TO setnum
    BOX 560;200-sn*10,24,8 COLOUR 1+sn FILL WITH 8
    MOVE 590;200-sn*10:PRINT sn
  NEXT sn
  RETURN

  LABEL piechart
  CLS
  RESTORE piechart
  FOR sn=1 TO setnum:READ howfar:NEXT sn
  FOR n=1 TO howfar:READ dummy:NEXT n
  DATA 4,6,10,16,24
```

```
DATA 180,340,100
DATA 140,200,100,490,100
DATA 110,320,135,120,70,510,70
DATA 100,200,150,440,150,120,50,520,50
DATA 90,140,150,500,150,320,100,140,50,500,50
READ radius
FOR sn=1 TO setnum
  READ x,y
  arcstart=0
  FOR gn=1 TO groupnum
    arcsize=group(sn,gn)/itemcount(sn)*360
    arcend=arcstart+arcsize
    ELLIPTICAL PIE x;y,radius,0.5,arcstart,arcend COLOUR gn FILL WITH 8
    arcstart=arcend
  NEXT gn
  MOVE x-4;y-4:PRINT sn
NEXT sn
FOR gn=1 TO groupnum
  BOX 8;200-gn*9,24,8 COLOUR gn FILL WITH 8
  PRINT AT(6;gn);head$(gn)
NEXT gn
GOSUB anykey
RETURN

LABEL exit
RETURN

LABEL anykey
PRINT AT (1;21);"Press any key to continue"
WHILE INKEY$="":WEND
RETURN
```

Chapter 3

Anagram Algorithms

While this program is primarily intended for crossword puzzlers, there are routines here that should be of interest to anyone who is interested in permutations. After all, an anagram is a permutation of a set of letters. The techniques developed here for generating all the possible arrangements of the letters should not be too difficult to transfer to other situations where you want to explore the alternative sequences of any given set of items.

Let's see how it works in crossword terms. A clue reads:

He might have me starring in circus (4−6)

Prior experience with the compiler's style tells you that *might* implies that the clue contains an anagram. You focus on *me starring* because it is a rather ungainly arrangement of words, and a quick count shows that they contain 10 letters − as many as are needed for the solution.

Using the *New Anagram* routine, you tell the program that you are looking for two words, and that the first is of four letters, the second of six. Then the letters to be used, *MESTARRING* are entered. If you now go direct to the *View Possibles* routine, the program will work out and display all the permutations of those ten letters. One of those will be the right answer. But a word of warning − there are over 3,600,000 possible permutations of ten letters! Even running at ten anagrams a second, it is going to take over four days to get through that lot.

The problem is that the possible permutations of a set is equal to the factorial of the number of items in the set. With three items, there are factorial 3 (often written 3!) or $3 \times 2 \times 1 = 6$ ways of arranging them. Thus ABC can be written ABC, ACB, BAC, BCA, CAB, CBA.

With four letters you can have 4! = 4 × 3 × 2 × 1 = 24 permutations:

ABCD	ABDC	ACBD	ACDB	ADBC	ADCB
BACD	BADC	BCAD	BCDA	BDAC	BDCA
CABD	CADB	CBAD	CBDA	CDAB	CDBA
DABC	DACB	DBAC	DBCA	DCAB	DCBA

By the time you get to seven letters, the possible permutations have shot up to 7! = 5040. The numbers start to get rather astronomic after that, so trying to solve 7 across − the 15-letter clue − can be a long, slow business!

However, the process can be speeded up significantly by fixing those letters that are known, leaving fewer to permutate. Hence the *Fix Letters* routine. And, in practice, once you start to view the possibles, the new arrangements of letters will suggest ideas, leading you to guess parts or the whole solution before the correct permutation has been reached.

To return to our earlier example, we might have found, by solving other clues, that the third letter of the first word is 'N' and that the second word starts with 'M' and its penultimate letter is 'E'. Looking again at the clue, it is a reasonable guess that the word ends '..ER':

   − − N −   M − − − E R

We are now left with only six letters *STARIG* − a mere 720 possible permutations. So, somewhere round the second screenful, if not before, you should have discovered that the answer is RING MASTER.

Program structure

Main loop

    Display menu
    Perform Options
    Until Exit selected

Options

    New Anagram − get solution layout   *newpara*
               and letters to be used

    Load Old Anagram − disk access   *loadpara*

    Save Current Anagram, layout and letters only   *savepara*

Fix Letters   *fixpara*
  Repeat
    Display layout, including letters already fixed
    Display free letters
    Get position of letter to fix
    If occupied, replace by dash and return that letter to pool
    Get letter to use and check that it is available
  Until no more letters known

View Possibles   *viewpara*
  Reset *slot()* array
  Repeat
    Drop letters into appropriate slots
    Display new arrangement
    Check for keyboard interruption
      – either 'Wait' or 'Stop'
    Adjust for next permutation   *roll*
  Until all possibles shown, or break in routine

Notes

Managing permutations

This posed a significant problem and had to be solved before the program could be written. How do you ensure that every letter has been tried in every possible position? In theory, setting positions with random numbers will eventually generate all possibilities, in the same way that a roomful number of monkeys with typewriters will eventually reproduce the Works of Shakespeare – given sufficient time. But that's in theory. Unless you are prepared to wait an awful long time for the last few new permutations, a more organised approach is essential.

Look at the part set of four-letter permutations shown in Table 3.1 and notice the pattern in the position values. The pattern is even more marked when you look at it in terms of 'Slot Availability'. By this I mean which of the available slots will a letter be placed in – remembering that as slots are occupied there are fewer left for the remaining letters. Take for example the third permutation 'ACBD', with the Slot pattern 1-2-1-1. The 'A' went into the first available slot:

A – – –

followed by the 'B' in the second empty slot that it came to:

A – B –

TABLE 3.1

Permutation	Position of letters				Slot availability			
	A	B	C	D	A	B	C	D
ABCD	1	2	3	4	1	1	1	1
ABDC	1	2	4	3	1	1	2	1
ACBD	1	3	2	4	1	2	1	1
ADBC	1	3	4	2	1	2	2	1
ACDB	1	4	2	3	1	3	1	1
ADCB	1	4	3	2	1	3	2	1
BACD	2	1	3	4	2	1	1	1
BADC	2	1	4	3	2	1	2	1

'C' is then slotted into the first available place:

A C B —

There remains only one possible place for 'D' to go.

With available spaces in *temp$* represented by dashes, we can use the INST function to count our way through the string to the place that we need. The value of this is held in the *slot* array. Hence, this routine in the *viewpara* section:

```
FOR loop=1 TO numletters-1
   find=0:startpoint=1
   REPEAT
      dash=INSTR(startpoint,temp$,"-")
      find=find+1
      startpoint=dash+1
   UNTIL find=slot(loop)
   MID$(temp$,dash,1)=MID$(letter$,loop,1)
NEXT loop
```

The pattern is then that the last letter will always go into the remaining free slot; the third letter alternates between free slots 1 and 2; the second between 1, 2 and 3; and the first will steadily work through from slot 1 to slot 4. This could be managed by a nest of loops:

```
FOR first = 1 TO 4
   FOR second = 1 TO 3
      FOR third = 1 TO 2
         word$(first) = letter$(1)
         word$(second) = letter$(2)
         word$(third) = letter$(3)
```

```
          empty = INSTR(word$,"-")
          word$(empty) = letter$(4)
          PRINT word$
      NEXT third
    NEXT second
  NEXT first
```

The nesting can be taken to whatever depth is required, but this system can be used only if you know in advance how many letters there will be in the set. Here we need a more flexible system. Let's go back to that Slot Availability pattern.

Notice how each letter cycles through a sequence; C goes from 1 to 2, then as it returns to 1, it trips the previous letter's cycle. When B reaches 3, the A cycle is incremented. It doesn't matter how many letters there are in the set; the actions are always the same:

Increment the current slot counter
  If past its limit, then
    reset to 1, make the prior counter current and loop back

This routine will make slot(0) 'current' and increment it when all the permutations have been produced. This, then, can be used as an exit check.

The *limit* will always be the number of letters in the set minus the current number plus one. Thus, for 'C', the third letter, the limit is $4 - 3 + 1 = 2$.

You can see the Basic implementation of this in the *roll* routine at the bottom of *viewpara*, where the current slot number is held in the *this* variable:

```
this=numletters-1
LABEL roll
slot(this)=slot(this)+1
IF slot(this)>numletters-this+1 THEN slot(this)=1:this=this-1:GOTO roll
```

It should be noticed that the *viewpara* routine always starts from scratch every time. You may wish to alter it so that if the routine has been interrupted — perhaps because of a lack of time to view all the possibles — it could be picked up from the breakpoint when it is next accessed. To do this, arrange for a flag to be set if the the routine is interrupted by an 'E' keypress; and at the start of *viewpara*, make the program flow leap over the lines that reset the *slot()* array if the breakflag is set.

The 'Fix Letters' Routine

When the program gets the position of the letter to fix, it makes sure that it is a valid position. Then, if there is a letter there already, that letter is removed from the solution layout and returned to the general pool:

```
REPEAT
  INPUT "Number of letter ";letnum
  this$=MID$(display$,letnum,1)
  UNTIL this$<>" " AND this$<>""    ("space" or "nothing")
  IF this$<>"-" THEN letter$=letter$+this$
```

Notice the flexibility of the MID$ function. It can slice any given number of letters out from the middle of a string:

```
this$ = MID$(display$,letnum,1)
```

takes a single character at the place identified by *letnum*. It can also serve in place of LEFT$ and RIGHT$ for slicing pieces off the ends; and where the slice is from the right-hand side, it is only necessary to give the starting place. All the characters from there onwards will be taken. Here, for example, a character is being removed from a string by chopping off both ends and sticking them back together:

```
letter$=MID$(letter$,1,inlet-1)+MID$(letter$,inlet+1)
```

MID$ can be used in the opposite way — for writing characters into existing strings. You don't have to specify how many, merely where to start. This line fixes the letter held in *here$* into the solution layout:

```
MID$(display$,letnum)=here$
```

If you prefer, the functions **MID$**, **LEFT$** and **RIGHT$** can all be replaced by subscripted string-slicing methods. In these, the sub-string is defined by position of the letters at the start and end. Thus, these two expressions are equivalent:

```
word$(3 TO 6)
```

and

```
MID$(word$,3,4)
```

Both slice off the four characters starting from the third in the string. Similarly

word$(5)	is equivalent to	MID$(word$,5)
word$(TO 4)	is equivalent to	LEFT$(word$,4)
word$(7 TO)	is equivalent to	RIGHT$(word$,LEN(word$)-6)

Note that if either the start or end value is omitted, Basic2 assumes that the left or right end of the string is wanted.

Disk storage

The program only saves and loads back the set of letters and the solution layout (including those letters already fixed). If you have altered the program as suggested above, so that the *viewpara* routine can pick up from the breakpoint , then you should extend the filing sections so that the *slot* array is also saved and reloaded.

Anagrams program

```
REM anagrams

SCREEN #1 TEXT 80 FIXED, 22 FIXED
WINDOW #1 FULL ON
DRIVE "B":REM please yourself which drive

DIM slot(50)

LABEL options
REPEAT
  CLS
  WINDOW CURSOR OFF
  PRINT "OPTION MENU"
  PRINT
  PRINT "NEW ANAGRAM......................1"
  PRINT "LOAD OLD ANAGRAM................2"
  PRINT "SAVE CURRENT ANAGRAM...........3"
  PRINT "FIX LETTERS....................4"
  PRINT "VIEW POSSIBLES.................5"
  PRINT "EXIT FROM PROGRAM.............6"
  REPEAT
    ky$=INKEY$
  UNTIL ky$>"0" AND ky$<"7"
  ky=VAL(ky$)
  IF ky<6 THEN ON ky GOSUB newpara,loadpara,savepara,fixpara,viewpara
UNTIL ky=6
END

LABEL newpara
CLS
WINDOW CURSOR ON
display$=""
total=0
INPUT "Number of Words ";numwords
FOR loop =1 TO numwords
```

```
   PRINT "Enter length of word ";loop
   INPUT wordlen
   total=total+wordlen
   display$=display$+STRING$(wordlen,"-")+" "
   PRINT display$
NEXT loop
display$=LEFT$(display$,total+numwords-1):REM crop off last space
REPEAT
   INPUT "Letters to be used ";letter$
   IF LEN(letter$)<>total THEN PRINT total;" letters are needed."
UNTIL LEN(letter$)=total
RETURN


LABEL loadpara
INPUT "Filename ";file$
OPEN #5 INPUT file$
INPUT #5,letter$
INPUT #5,display$
CLOSE 5
RETURN


LABEL savepara
INPUT "Filename for saving ";file$
OPEN #5 OUTPUT file$
PRINT #5,letter$
PRINT #5 display$
CLOSE 5
RETURN


LABEL fixpara
REPEAT
  CLS
  FOR loop=1 TO LEN(display$)
    PRINT AT(loop*2+1;2);MID$(display$,loop,1)
    PRINT AT(loop*2;4);loop
  NEXT loop
  PRINT AT(1;6);"Possible letters ";letter$
  REPEAT
    INPUT AT(1;8);"Position number ";letnum
    this$=MID$(display$,letnum,1)
  UNTIL this$<>" " AND this$<>""
   REM check for valid position
   IF this$<>"-" THEN letter$=letter$+this$
   REM put letter back in pool
   inlet=0
   WHILE inlet=0
```

43

```
      INPUT AT(1;10);"Letter to go here ";here$
      inlet=INSTR(1,letter$,here$)
      IF inlet=0 THEN PRINT "Not Possible!"
    WEND
    MID$(display$,letnum)=here$
    letter$=MID$(letter$,1,inlet-1)+MID$(letter$,inlet+1)
     REM cut out used letter and close gap
    PRINT AT(letnum*2+1;2);here$
    INPUT AT(1;15);"Any more? (Y/N)",again$
  UNTIL UPPER$(again$)="N"
  RETURN


  LABEL viewpara
  numletters=LEN(letter$)
  slot(0)=0
  FOR loop=1 TO numletters-1
    slot(loop)=1
  NEXT loop


  REPEAT
    temp$=display$
     REM slot letters into place
    FOR loop=1 TO numletters-1
      find=0:startpoint=1
      REPEAT
        dash=INSTR(startpoint,temp$,"-")
        find=find+1
        startpoint=dash+1
      UNTIL find=slot(loop)
      MID$(temp$,dash,1)=MID$(letter$,loop,1)
    NEXT loop
     REM remaining letter
    dash=INSTR(temp$,"-")
    MID$(temp$,dash,1)=MID$(letter$,numletters)
    PRINT temp$,
     REM get next permutation
    this=numletters-1

    LABEL roll
    slot(this)=slot(this)+1
    IF slot(this)>numletters-this+1 THEN slot(this)=1:this=this-1:GOTO roll
    ky$=UPPER$(INKEY$)
    IF ky$="W" THEN PRINT "Waiting":GOSUB spacebar
  UNTIL slot(0)=1 OR ky$="E"
  IF slot(0)=1 THEN PRINT "All permutations shown"
  GOSUB spacebar
```

```
RETURN

LABEL spacebar
PRINT "Press spacebar to continue"
REPEAT
  ky$=INKEY$
UNTIL ky$=" "
RETURN
```

Chapter 4

Security by Scrambling

Although this program is about the protection of files, it has been included in this section because it demonstrates some key aspects of text handling.

If you have files that you need to keep secure from prying eyes, the DOS system does not offer much protection. You can conceal the nature of files by using misleading names − MYTHING is less obvious that ACCOUNTS.DAT − but will only deter the most casual peeker. File names can be made more unreadable by using the Extended ASCII set − those produced by holding down ALT and typing their numbers; and the blank characters are particularly valuable in this respect. But again, this is little more than an irritant to the determined hacker.

A far higher level of security can be obtained through the CP/M password protection system, but in practice this does not fit well with Basic programs. There is nothing to stop you from using the CP/M format for Basic disks and setting passwords and protection for Basic files, but this can only be done under DOS Plus, not from within Basic. Any Basic application that used CP/M protection would impose unreasonable demands upon its users. Any files that were to be accessed during a working session would have to be unprotected at the start, before switching to the GEM/Basic system and running the program, then have their protection restored at the end!

Here then is an alternative, and far simpler, method of rendering a text file secure. It provides a double level of protection; only those who know the password will be able to gain access to a file from within a program, and the file contents are scrambled so that they will be meaningless if read by the DOS Plus **TYPE** or **PIP** commands.

Putting a password on a file is easily done. It is just written in as the first item on the file. Then, when the file is opened again later for reading, the stored password will be compared with the one given by the user. If they fail to match, the file will be closed.

Scrambling is a little more involved, and involves a variety of encryption. Did you ever, as a child, use those codes where one letter stands for another? The simplest types of these worked by displacing the alphabet a set number of letters one way or the other.

CODED   XYZABCDEFGHIJKLMNOPQRSTUVX
CLEAR   ABCDEFGHIJKLMNOPQRSTUVWXYZ

Here, for example, the coded word 'JFZOL' means 'MICRO'. This type of code is easy to crack by letter-frequency and word-shape analysis. There are patterns that crop up in any message of more than a few sentences. For a start, if this was written in English, we would probably find several occurrences of the single character 'X', suggesting that this must stand for 'A'; and that 'B' is the most common letter, and presumably stands for 'E' − the most common letter in English. Try a displacement of three to the left and the coded message is broken instantly.

A more secure code can be had if the displacement is altered after each letter. Encryption wheels are sometimes used for this purpose. They consist of two circles of card, one slightly smaller than the other, with the alphabet and digits are arranged around the circumference of each. To encode or decode a message, one wheel is turned, in a known sequence, after each letter. If you do not know the sequence, it is extremely difficult to decode such a message. Frequency analysis will get you nowhere as no single letter stands for any other.

It is a variety of this method that is used in 'Scrambler'. Here, the ASCII codes of the password characters are used for the sequence of displacements. Each in turn is added to the ASCII codes of the file's characters. When the end of the password is reached, then the sequence starts again from the beginning. For example, take the four-letter password 'MOLE' − ASCII codes 77 79 76 69 − and a piece of text that begins 'THE SECRET SERVICE..'. Table 4.1 shows how they would be combined.

TABLE 4.1

	T	H	E	S	E	C	R	E	T	S	E	R	V	I	C	E
CLEAR	84	72	69	83	69	67	82	69	84	83	69	82	86	73	67	69
+ KEY	77	79	76	69	77	79	76	69	77	79	76	69	77	79	76	69
CODED	161	151	145	152	146	146	158	138	161	162	145	151	163	152	143	138

The resultant ASCII codes are, of course beyond the normal text range, so the file will appear as a jumble of special characters and block graphics which will deter the casual peeker. But even if you take the coded file in ASCII number form, there is no pattern to the codes. Notice how the five occurrences of the letter 'E' are represented variously by 145, 146 and 138; and that 151 stands for 'H' on one occasion and 'R' on another.

You can see how this process is translated into Basic in the *write* routine of the program. Notice also that a variation on this is used for scrambling the password at the start of the file. If the password's ASCII codes were simply added to themselves, then it could be decoded by anyone who knew how the system worked. All they would need to do to find the password would be to divide the first few numbers by 2! Instead, the *passkey* array — the sequence of ASCII codes — is reversed for scrambling the password.

The scrambling program

```
REM scramble

SCREEN #1 TEXT 80 FIXED,20 FIXED
WINDOW #1 FULL ON
WINDOW #1 CURSOR ON
DRIVE "B"

REPEAT
  PRINT "Scrambler"
  INPUT "Write file, Read file or Exit (W/R/E) ";opt$
  IF UPPER$(opt$)="W" THEN GOSUB write
  IF UPPER$(opt$)="R" THEN GOSUB reader
UNTIL UPPER$(opt$)="E"
END

LABEL write
GOSUB filename
over$="N"
WHILE file$=x$ AND over$="N"
  INPUT "File exists. Overwrite? (Y/N) ",over$
  IF UPPER$(over$)="N" THEN GOSUB filename
WEND
OPEN #5 OUTPUT file$
pass$=""
WHILE LEN (pass$)<>6
  INPUT "Password for this file (6 letters) ";pass$
WEND
FOR n=1 TO 6
  passkey(n)=ASC(MID$(pass$,n,1))
NEXT n
count=6
FOR n=1 to 6
  letternum=ASC(MID$(pass$,n,1))
  letternum=letternum+passkey(count)
```

```
    MID$(pass$,n,1)=CHR$(letternum)
    count=count-1
NEXT n
PRINT #5,pass$
INPUT "Data for Filing ";data$
WHILE data$<>""
count=1
FOR n=1 TO LEN(data$)
    letternum=ASC(MID$(data$,n,1))
    letternum=(letternum+passkey(count))
    MID$(data$,n,1)=CHR$(letternum)
    count=count+1:IF count=7 THEN count=1
NEXT n
PRINT #5,data$
INPUT "Data for filing ";data$
WEND
CLOSE #5
RETURN

LABEL reader
GOSUB filename
WHILE x$<>file$
    PRINT "No such file on disk. "
    GOSUB filename
WEND
OPEN #5 INPUT file$
pass$=""
WHILE LEN (pass$)<>6
    INPUT "Password for this file (6 letters) ";pass$
WEND
FOR n=1 TO 6
    passkey(n)=ASC(MID$(pass$,n,1))
NEXT n
INPUT #5,data$
count=6
FOR n=1 TO 6
    letternum=ASC(MID$(data$,n,1))
    letternum=letternum-passkey(count)
    MID$(data$,n,1)=CHR$(letternum)
count=count-1
NEXT n
IF data$<>pass$ THEN PRINT "Wrong password.":CLOSE #5:RETURN
PRINT "Welcome to ";file$
WHILE NOT EOF (#5)
    INPUT #5,data$
    count=1
```

```
  FOR n=1 TO LEN(data$)
    letternum=ASC(MID$(data$,n,1))
    letternum=(letternum-passkey(count))
    MID$(data$,n,1)=CHR$(letternum)
    count=count+1:IF count=7 THEN count=1
  NEXT n
  PRINT data$
WEND
CLOSE #5
RETURN

LABEL filename
INPUT "Filename ";file$
WHILE LEN(file$)<8:file$=file$+" ":WEND
IF LEN(file$)>8 THEN file$=LEFT$(file$,8)
file$=UPPER$(file$)+".EXT":REM add own extension
PRINT "Filename is ";file$
x$=FIND$(file$)
RETURN
```

PART 2

FILES AND DIRECTORIES

Chapter 5

Telephone Book and Timer

As this section is about files and directories, it seems appropriate to start with a telephone directory system! And this one can also be used to time and price any call that is made.

When the program is run, the directory is loaded from the file into memory and space allocated for up to 50 new entries. The charge rates are also loaded in at this point. On exit, the data is rewritten onto disk if any alterations have been made. As the names and numbers are in memory, rather than on disk, during the course of the program, finding a number and re-organising the data are both accomplished quickly.

There are only five main options. The whole directory can be listed, either on paper or on the screen; entries can be added or removed; a specific number can be looked up – with the time/cost option arising out of this; and charge rates can be set. This last routine must be run before the time/cost routine is accessed.

When looking up a name, either to delete the entry or to find the number, a list of surnames can be called up in a second window. If there are more than 20 names, this list will be longer than the visible screen, but the normal GEM system can be used to drag the window up or down the list to locate a name.

As designed, the program will work out costs on normal inland telephone calls. If you wish to include overseas or mobile telephone numbers in your directory, then the charge arrays and routines will need to be expanded to cater for these.

Program structure

Initialisation

> Screen
> Rates array
> Check disk for file then
> > Either load file   *loader*
> > Or set up for new start   *newstart*

Main loop

> Display menu
> Perform options
> Until done
> Exit − save file if changes have been made   *exit*

Options

> List entries
> > Either to screen   *screenout*
> > Or to paper   *printout*
>
> Add an entry
> > Get details: Name, address, Tel No, band   *add*
> > Sort into order
> > Until no more new entries
> > Set flag for saving
>
> Delete an entry   *deleter*
> > Get name   *lookup*
> > Check before deleting
> > Set flag for saving
>
> Find a number   *find*
> > Get name   *lookup*
> > Display number and rate   *getrate*
> > If wanted, run timer and show cost   *showcost*
>
> Set charge rates   *setrates*
> > Set flag for saving

Notes

Disk files

The program generates a file called TELEFONE.DAT − note the use of the .DAT extension to distinguish this from the program. The file has a simple sequential structure:

    Number of entries
    For every record
        surname (or company name)
        other name(s)
        address
        telephone number
        charge band (local, A, B1 or B)
    Table of charge rates

In the *startup* routine, the command

```
x$=FIND$("TELEFONE.DAT")
```

searches the disk for a matching file. If found, *x$* will take the value TELEFONE.DAT and a check on this will tell the program whether or not to prepare for a new file or load an existing one. It is not obvious from this usage, but **FIND$** is a direct equivalent to the DOS **DIR** command. The file specification can be given in lower or upper case, does not have to be formatted to the eight letters plus three-letter extension standard and may include wildcards. We will return to FIND$ in the next program, where it plays a more active role.

List entries

While most of the programs in this set use a single routine for outputting lists and controlling the direction of output by setting the stream number, this one has two separate routines for listing on screen and paper.

The *printout* routine simply runs through a loop, sending records to the printer using the **LPRINT** command. The presentation could well be improved. Details could be printed in neat columns by using the **TAB** function:

```
LPRINT surname$(loop);TAB(15);name$(loop);TAB(30);address$(loop)....
```

The columns could be headed up to match. Where there is more than a single page of entries, then add a line to print a form-feed and new headings after every 60 entries:

```
IF loop MOD 60=0 THEN LPRINT CHR$(12):LPRINT "SURNAME.....
```

The *screenout* routine could be adapted in a similar way, so that after every 20 entries had been displayed the program would wait for a keypress. As it stands, the list will scroll steadily past until the ESCape key is pressed. The **INKEY** function is used to test for this. As it returns key codes, rather than character values, INKEY can be used on the whole keyboard, and is executed more quickly. The other two control keys are tested within the Escape test loop − 13 is the code for both the L-shaped Return key and the numberpad Enter; 335 is the code for End:

```
WHILE INKEY=27
   PRINT "Press [Enter] to restart, [End] to abort"
   REPEAT
     ky=INKEY
   UNTIL ky=13 or ky=335
   IF ky=335 then loop=current
WEND
```

Add an entry and sort into order

This program uses the simplest possible system for keeping the file in alphabetical order. It never lets it get out of order! When a new entry is added, it is initially put into the last position. Then the routine checks through the file to find the first surname that should come after the new one. All of the records from that one to the end are then shuffled down one position, and finally, the new entry is brought up into the space that has been created for it, and erased from its temporary position − see Table 5.1.

TABLE 5.1

	Step 1		Step 2	Step 3
	ALLENS		ALLENS	ALLENS
	BROWN		BROWN	BROWN
	GREEN	Here>	GREEN	DAVIES
	SMITH		GREEN	GREEN
New>	DAVIES		SMITH	SMITH
	-----		DAVIES	-----

Note that in Step 2 the loop runs from the bottom of the list back up to the insert point:

```
FOR loop=current TO this STEP -1
surname$(loop)=surname$(loop-1)

....
```

Delete an entry

This uses a variation on the sort routine to close up the gap created by removing an entry:

```
FOR loop=this TO current
surname$(loop)=surname$(loop+1)
....
```

This is a crude but effective solution to the problem of keeping files in order. With a relatively small file, it doesn't take very long to shuffle a set of records up or down one place. Indeed, until you have got more than 50 or so entries, you will be scarcely aware of the delay while the file is re-organised. However, with larger files, you may need a quicker and more efficient means of ordering the records. In this event, the routines should be rewritten so that the arrays are handled as *linked lists*. An explanation of how these work is given in the next chapter.

The 'Lookup' routine

This is used by both *deleter* and *find*. When a surname is keyed in it is converted to upper case, then compared with those in the surname$ array to find the record number. This will be stored in the variable *this*. Now, as it stands, the surname must be typed in exactly as contained in the array — ignoring case only. The system would be quicker and easier to use if it were possible to type in just the first few characters of a name. This can be managed in several ways. The INSTR function can search for a match of any set of characters within a string:

```
FOR loop=1 TO current
found=INSTR(surname$(loop),temp$)
IF found>0 THEN this=loop:loop=current
```

A little forethought is needed here. With the check defined as *found>0*, this will set the *this* flag wherever the match is inside the string. So, if you were looking for 'The Pearly Gates Chinese Restaurant', and keyed in 'Pearly', the routine would locate the correct telephone number. Against that, if you wanted the number of 'Wright Brothers' and typed 'Wright', you could be given the Cartwright's number instead. By altering the check to read *found=1* you would prevent this, but would lose the facility for giving part-names from within the string.

The *Directory* Routine can be accessed from *lookup* when the user wants to scan through the directory. Window #2 is defined as a TEXT FLEXIBLE screen, with a narrow visible area. As such, the screen will hold 2000 characters — considerably more than can be displayed in the window. When the surnames are printed on it, by a simple loop, only the first 20 will be visible initially, but the rest can be viewed by pulling the screen down the window. That 2000-character limit means that, with a visible width of 20 characters, up to 100 entries can be held. If your directory has more entries than this, then use a narrower window to get more length and trim the surnames to fit:

```
WINDOW #2 SIZE 10,20
FOR loop=1 TO entries
PRINT #2, LEFT$(surname$(loop),10)
NEXT loop
```

Timing and costing a call

All direct dialled calls are costed in the same way; 5p (at current prices) for each whole or part time-unit that is used. The length of a time-unit depends upon the time-of-day *rate* − cheap, standard or peak, and the distance *band* − Local, A, B1 or B. The charge band must written in when an entry is made, but the time-of-day rate can be calculated by the program using the **TIME** and **DATE** functions.

TIME tells you the number of hundredths of a second that have elapsed since the start of the day. This value is converted into hours by a sequence of integer divisions, then checked to see if it falls within the peak or cheap rate limits:

```
sec=TIME\100
mins=sec\60
hrs=mins\60
rate=cheap
IF hrs>=8 OR hrs<18 THEN rate=standard
IF hrs>=9 AND hrs<13 THEN rate=peak
```

Weekends are all cheap rate, so we need to check the day. DATE returns the number of days since the start of the century. Modulo division on this will give the day number, where 0 is Sunday and 6 is Saturday:

```
day=DATE MOD 7
IF day=0 OR day=6 THEN rate=cheap
```

Given that the *charge* array contains a table of time units, arranged by distance band and rates, the relevant one is easily picked out:

```
IF code$(this)="A" THEN units=charge(rate,2)
```

Telephone system program

```
REM Telephone System

DRIVE "B"
SCREEN #1 TEXT 80 FIXED,22 FIXED
WINDOW #1 TITLE "TELEPHONE BOOK"
WINDOW #1 FULL ON
savefile=0

LABEL startup
REM set up rates array
rate$(1)="CHEAP":rate$(2)="STANDARD":rate$(3)="PEAK"
band$(1)="Local":band$(2)="A":band$(3)="B1":band$(4)="B"
DIM charge(3,4)


x$=FIND$("TELEFONE.DAT")
IF x$<>"TELEFONE.DAT" THEN GOSUB newstart ELSE GOSUB loader

LABEL options
REPEAT
  CLS
  PRINT "Telephone System Options"
  PRINT
  PRINT "List entries...............1"
  PRINT "Add an entry...............2"
  PRINT "Delete an entry............3"
  PRINT "Find a number..............4"
  PRINT "Set Charge Rates...........5"
  PRINT "Exit from program..........6"

  REPEAT
    opt$=INKEY$
  UNTIL opt$>="1"AND opt$<="6"
  ON VAL(opt$) GOSUB list,add,deleter,find,setrates,exit
UNTIL opt$="6"
END


LABEL loader
OPEN #5 INPUT "TELEFONE.DAT"
PRINT "Loading data from disk. Please wait"
INPUT #5,entries
current=entries+1
num=entries+50
DIM surname$(num),name$(num),address$(num),number$(num),code$(num)
```

```
FOR loop=1 TO entries
  INPUT #5,surname$(loop)
  INPUT #5,name$(loop)
  INPUT #5,address$(loop)
  INPUT #5,number$(loop)
  INPUT #5,code$(loop)
NEXT loop

INPUT #5,unitcharge
FOR rate=1 TO 3
  FOR band=1 TO 4
    INPUT #5,charge(rate,band)
  NEXT band
NEXT rate

CLOSE 5
RETURN


LABEL newstart
entries=0
current=1
num=50
DIM surname$(num),name$(num),address$(num),number$(num),code$(num)
GOSUB setrates
RETURN

LABEL list
CLS
PRINT "Output to screen or paper (S/P) "
REPEAT
  a$=UPPER$(INKEY$)
UNTIL a$="S" OR a$="P"
IF a$="S" THEN GOSUB screenout ELSE GOSUB printout
RETURN

LABEL screenout
PRINT "Press [Escape] to halt display"
FOR loop=1 TO current-1
  PRINT
  PRINT name$(loop),surname$(loop),address$(loop),number$(loop)

  WHILE INKEY=27
    PRINT "Press [Enter] to restart, [End] to abort"
    REPEAT
      ky=INKEY
```

```
    UNTIL ky=13 OR ky=335
     IF ky=335 THEN loop=current
   WEND

NEXT loop
PRINT "End of list."
GOSUB anykey
RETURN

LABEL printout
LPRINT "Telephone System Entries"
LPRINT
FOR loop=1 TO current-1
   LPRINT name$(loop),surname$(loop),address$(loop),number$(loop)
NEXT loop
RETURN

LABEL add
REPEAT
  CLS
  PRINT "New Entry"
  PRINT
  INPUT "Surname or Company Name";a$
  surname$(current)=UPPER$(a$)
  INPUT "Other names ";name$(current)
  INPUT "Address ";address$(current)
  INPUT "Number ";number$(current)
  INPUT "Charge Band (Local, A, B1, B)";a$
  code$(current)=UPPER$(a$)
  current=current+1

  IF current=2 THEN GOTO nextentry

  REM sorting - may be omitted
  PRINT "Sorting into order. Please wait"
  this=0
  FOR loop=1 TO current-2
    IF surname$(current-1)<surname$(loop) THEN this=loop:loop=current
  NEXT loop
  IF this=0 THEN GOTO nextentry

  REM shuffle list down a place
  FOR loop=current TO this STEP -1
    surname$(loop)=surname$(loop-1)
    name$(loop)=name$(loop-1)
    address$(loop)=address$(loop-1)
```

```
    number$(loop)=number$(loop-1)
    code$(loop)=code$(loop-1)
  NEXT loop

  REM transfer new entry to sorted position
  surname$(this)=surname$(current)
  name$(this)=name$(current)
  address$(this)=address$(current)
  number$(this)=number$(current)
  code$(this)=code$(current)
  surname$(current)=""
  name$(current)=""

  LABEL nextentry
  PRINT "Another entry? (Y/N)"
  GOSUB yesno
UNTIL a$="N"
savefile=1
RETURN

LABEL deleter
GOSUB lookup
PRINT AT(2;12);"Are you sure you want to delete this? (Y/N)"
GOSUB yesno
IF a$="N" THEN RETURN

REM shuffle entries up to close gap
FOR loop=this TO current
  surname$(loop)=surname$(loop+1)
  name$(loop)=name$(loop+1)
  address$(loop)=address$(loop+1)
  number$(loop)=number$(loop+1)
  code$(loop)=code$(loop+1)
NEXT loop
current=current-1
savefile=1
RETURN

LABEL find
this=0
GOSUB lookup
IF this=0 THEN RETURN
CLS
PRINT "The number for ";name$(this);" ";surname$(this)
PRINT " is ";number$(this)
GOSUB getrate
```

```
PRINT "You get ";units;" seconds per ";unitcharge;"p. just now."
PRINT
PRINT "Do you want to time and price this call? (Y/N)"
GOSUB yesno
IF a$="N" THEN GOSUB anykey:RETURN

PRINT "Press [S] to start the timer; [E] to end."

ky$=UPPER$(INKEY$)
WHILE ky$<>"S"
  ky$=UPPER$(INKEY$)
WEND
starttime=TIME\100

used=1:GOSUB showcost

WHILE ky$<>"E"
  unittime=TIME\100-starttime
  temp=unittime\units+1
  IF temp<>used THEN used=temp:GOSUB showcost
  ky$=UPPER$(INKEY$)
WEND

GOSUB anykey
RETURN

LABEL showcost
cost=used*unitcharge
PRINT AT(2;10);"The cost of this call..."
PRINT AT(6;12);"....[po]";ROUND(cost/100,2)
RETURN

LABEL lookup
dirflag=0
CLS
PRINT "Press [D] to open Directory Window"
PRINT "Any other key to enter name."
ky$=""
WHILE ky$=""
  ky$=UPPER$(INKEY$)
WEND
IF ky$="D" THEN GOSUB directory
INPUT "Surname or Company name ";name$
name$=UPPER$(name$)
FOR loop=1 TO entries
  IF surname$(loop)=name$ THEN this=loop:loop=entries
```

63

```
NEXT loop
IF this=0 THEN PRINT "Sorry, no entry for that name":GOSUB anykey
IF dirflag=1 THEN WINDOW #2 CLOSE
RETURN

LABEL directory
dirflag=1
SCREEN #2 TEXT FLEXIBLE
WINDOW #2 CLOSE
WINDOW #2 SIZE 20,22
WINDOW #2 PLACE 440;100
WINDOW #2 TITLE "Any Key to Exit"
WINDOW #2 OPEN
FOR loop=1 TO entries
  PRINT #2,surname$(loop)
NEXT loop
ky$=""
WHILE ky$=""
  ky$=INKEY$
WEND
RETURN

LABEL getrate
cheap=1
standard=2
peak=3
sec=TIME\100
mins=sec\60
hrs=mins\60
rate=cheap
IF hrs>=8 AND hrs<18 THEN rate=standard
IF hrs>=9 AND hrs<13 THEN rate=peak
day=DATE MOD 7
IF day=0 OR day=6 THEN rate=cheap

units=charge(rate,1)
IF code$(this)="A" THEN units=charge(rate,2)
IF code$(this)="B1" THEN units=charge(rate,3)
IF code$(this)="B" THEN units=charge(rate,4)
RETURN

LABEL setrates
CLS
INPUT "Current charge per unit ";unitcharge
FOR rate=1 TO 3
  PRINT rate$(rate);" RATE CALLS"
```

```
    PRINT "Seconds per Unit"
    FOR band=1 TO 4
      PRINT "Charge Band ";band$(band)
      INPUT charge(rate,band)
    NEXT band
  NEXT rate
  savefile=1
  RETURN

  LABEL yesno
  REPEAT
    a$=UPPER$(INKEY$)
  UNTIL a$="Y" OR a$="N"
  RETURN

  LABEL anykey
  PRINT "Press any key to return to menu"
  a$=INKEY$
  WHILE a$=""
    a$=INKEY$
  WEND
  RETURN

  LABEL exit
  IF savefile=0 THEN RETURN
  OPEN #5 OUTPUT "TELEFONE.DAT"
  PRINT "Saving data to disk. Please wait"
  entries=current-1
  PRINT #5,entries
  FOR loop=1 TO entries
    PRINT #5,surname$(loop)
    PRINT #5,name$(loop)
    PRINT #5,address$(loop)
    PRINT #5,number$(loop)
    PRINT #5,code$(loop)
  NEXT loop
  PRINT #5,unitcharge
  FOR rate=1 TO 3
    FOR band = 1 TO 4
      PRINT #5,charge(rate,band)
    NEXT band
  NEXT rate
  CLOSE 5
  RETURN
```

Chapter 6

Jotter

This program is intended to provide a convenient means of handling notes and jottings. It is not a word processor, but could be thought of as a simple ideas processor. In terms of Basic2 programming it demonstrates file and directory functions and the management of linked lists.

Each file created by the program will be a set of up to 100 jottings. The only limitations on the size of these are that each jotting is a single string. The intention is that the jotter should be used as a flexible notepad. Jot down ideas as they come to you, then pull them into shape later by re-ordering them, deleting or inserting new ones, or making some stand out as headings.

The 'List files on disk' option will search the disk for any files that have the distinctive .JOT extension, then display on screen the file name, the number of jottings and the start of the first entry — in case you have forgotten what it was all about.

Program structure

Main loop

Display menu
Perform options
Until exit
— save current file if necessary

Options

    Create new file
        Get name and check for existing one
        Set up list and pointers
        Take notes in sequence until done or full list

    Edit loop
        Display menu
        Perform options
            Display notes
                Find where
                If to screen, hold at end of each page
            Change a jotting − identified by number
            Insert new jotting into list
            Delete old jotting
            Move jotting to new position
            Make jotting into heading by capitalising

    Print file using 'Display notes' routine directed to printer

    Load file
        Get and check filename
        Prepare list and pointers
        Read in jottings

    Save file − write jottings to disk in numerical order

    List all files
        Search disk for .JOT endings
        Display name, size and first entry of each

    Delete file using KILL command

    Rename file
        Get and check new filename
        Use NAME command

Notes

Linked lists

In the telephone book program (Chapter 5) the records were held in memory in a simple array structure. If you have used that program and built up a sizeable directory, you will have noticed that re-organising the file, whether to slot a new entry into place or to delete an unwanted number, takes a moment or two. This is inevitable, as any re-organisation involves moving data within the array. Delete the first entry from a 100-record directory and 99 records must be shuffled up a place.

With a linked list no data is actually moved when re-organising the list. Each item has a *pointer* which holds the number of the next item; by altering the pointers, you can insert, delete or move the items. The list is held in an array, with each item location being a subscript. The pointers are held in a matching array. Let's work through an example to see how the list is managed. Here someone is planning their weekend chores.

TABLE 6.1

No.	Item (Note$)	Pointer
0		1
1		2
2		3
3		4
4		5
5		6
6		7
..		..

When the list is initialised, the pointers link each empty item space to the next in a simple series as shown in Table 6.1. After the first entries have been made, the end of the list is marked by setting the end pointer to -1, and the location of the first empty space is held in a variable called *freespace*. Notice that location 0 is left blank. This allows us to use a single routine for inserting new entries. They are always inserted AFTER a given number, so to put something at the start of the list, we can simply 'Insert after 0'.

TABLE 6.2

No.	Item (Note$)	Pointer
0		1
1	Cut lawn	2
2	Tidy greenhouse	3
3	Wash car	4
4	Buy & plant roses	-1
5		6
6		7
..		..

freespace = 5

68

The list is completed (see Table 6.2). Pointer 4 is set to −1 to mark the end, and *freespace* is set to 5. Later our gardening friend remembers that he wanted to put up new shelves in the greenhouse, and that he should do this job as soon as it is tidy. So the new jotting is to be inserted after 2. The list now looks like Table 6.3.

TABLE 6.3

No.	Item (Note$)	Pointer
0		1
1	Cut lawn	2
2	Tidy greenhouse	5
3	Wash car	4
4	Buy & plant roses	-1
5	Put up shelves	3
6		7
..		..

freespace = 6

When the list is printed out, it will follow the pointers to give:

```
start at pointer(0)      1
    1  Cut lawn          2
    2  Tidy greenhouse   5
    5  Put up shelves    3
    3  Wash car          4
    4  Buy & plant roses  -1  stop
```

Notice how pointer 2 (Tidy greenhouse) links to 5 (Put up shelves), and the pointer there takes the flow back to 3. The end-of-list marker stays where it was, but *freespace* is now 6.

You can see how this is managed in this section of the *injot* routine. The variable *jot* holds the number of the jotting after which the new one is to be inserted:

```
empty=freespace
freespace=pointer(freespace)
pointer(empty)=pointer(jot)
pointer(jot)=empty
INPUT "Jotting to be inserted ";note$(empty)
```

Variable	Initial values	Values after processing
freespace	5	6
pointer(5)	6	3
pointer(2)	3	5

TABLE 6.4

No.	Item (Note$)	Pointer
0		2
1	Cut lawn	6
2	Tidy greenhouse	5
3	Wash car	4
4	Buy & plant roses	-1
5	Put up shelves	3
6		7
..		..

freespace = 1

As the weekend draws near, the gardener decides that the lawn can be left for a few days, so that job can be crossed out — delete note 1 (see Table 6.4). 'Cut lawn' is not physically removed, but that location is now treated as the first 'free space', and when the list is printed the pointer trail leaps over it:

```
start at pointer(0)        2
   2  Tidy greenhouse       5
   5  Put up shelves        3
   3  Wash car              4
   4  Buy & plant roses    -1  stop
```

The pointer that had led to 'Cut lawn' now takes the flow to the next item and the location has been drawn into 'free space'. Next time a new item is inserted, it will go into location 1.

Here are the key lines from the *deletejot* routine. This time *jot* holds the number of the item to be removed:

```
GOSUB findpointer
pointer(this)=pointer(jot)
pointer(jot)=freespace
freespace=jot
```

The *findpointer* subroutine scans through the pointer array until it finds the one that

70

contains the number of the location to be deleted. The number is returned in *this*.

Variable	Initial values	Values after processing
freespace	6	1
pointer(0)	1	2
pointer(2)	3	6

Re-ordering the list does not involve any movement of actual data, any more than deletion requires the removal of data. Once again it is all done with the pointers (see Table 6.5).

TABLE 6.5

No.	Item (Note$)	Pointer
0		2
1		6
2	Tidy greenhouse	5
3	Wash car	-1
4	Buy & plant roses	3
5	Put up shelves	4
6		7
..		..

freespace = 1

As it happens, this has brought 'Wash car' to the end of the list, so the −1 end flag has been moved to its pointer. The apparent disorder in the pointer array resolves into a properly organised printed list:

```
start at pointer(0)    2
   2  Tidy greenhouse    5
   5  Put up shelves     4
   4  Buy & plant roses  3
   3  Wash car          -1 stop
```

The *movejot* routine starts by getting the number of the jotting to be moved in the variable *jot*. The *findpointer* subroutine is brought into play again as it was in *deletejot*:

```
GOSUB findpointer
pointer(this)=pointer(jot)
INPUT "Insert after which Jotting ";after
pointer(jot)=pointer(after)
pointer(after)=jot
```

When working on this program you may wish to add an extra routine to print out the note$ and pointer arrays in their normal order so that you can see more clearly how the linked list works.

The system can be used in any program where you have lists that need to be re-organised and where the extra speed of linked lists would be valuable. In 'Jotter' we are only using one data array, but the technique can be easily extended to work with a set of arrays. The Telephone Book, for example, could be rewritten to use linked lists, as shown in Table 6.6.

TABLE 6.6

Num.	Name	Address	Tel. No.	Code	Pointer
0					1
1					2
2					3
..					..

With several arrays, the pointers refer to all items in the same line right across the set. As it is only ever the pointers that are changed during re-organisations, the number and size of data arrays is irrelevant. Indeed, the benefits of linked lists will be more obvious where there are large quantities of data and large numbers of arrays.

Disk management via Basic

The *lister*, *killer* and *rename* routines towards the end of the program demonstrate the use of the Basic2 disk management commands **FIND$**, **KILL** and **NAME**.

FIND$ is the DIR equivalent, but with added features:

```
file$=FIND$("*.JOT",flag)
```

This allows us to work through all the files on the disk with a .JOT extension. The *flag* specifies which filename to read into *file$*. If *flag* held 3, then it would be the third .JOT file that was accessed. So, by incrementing *flag*, we can take the files one at a time, in their disk order.

KILL is identical to the DOS command, ERASE.

NAME is virtually the same as RENAME, but slightly more readable:

NAME oldfile$ AS newfile$

Jotter program

```
REM jotter

SCREEN #1 TEXT 80 FIXED,22 FIXED
WINDOW #1 FULL ON
WINDOW CURSOR ON

DIM note$(100),pointer(100)

LABEL menu

REPEAT
  outwhere=1
   REM normally list to screen

  CLS
  PRINT "JOTTER OPTIONS"
  PRINT
  PRINT "Create New File ..........1"
  PRINT "Edit Current File ........2"
  PRINT "Print Out ................3"
  PRINT "Load Old File ............4"
  PRINT "Save Current File ........5"
  PRINT "List Files on Disk .......6"
  PRINT "Delete Disk File .........7"
  PRINT "Rename Disk File ........8"
  PRINT "Exit from Program ........9"

  REPEAT
    ky$=INKEY$
  UNTIL ky$>="1" AND ky$<="9"
  ky=VAL(ky$)
  ON ky GOSUB create,editor,printer,loader,saver,lister,killer,rename,exit
UNTIL ky$="9"
END

LABEL create
REPEAT
  CLS
  INPUT "Name of New File ";filename$
  filename$=UPPER$(filename$)+"          "
  filename$=LEFT$(filename$,8)+".JOT"
  x$=FIND$(filename$)
  IF x$=filename$ THEN PRINT "File already exists."
UNTIL x$<>filename$
```

```
active=0
FOR loop=0 TO 100
  note$(loop)=""
  pointer(loop)=loop+1
NEXT loop
pointer(100)=0
freespace=1

PRINT "Starting new file."
PRINT "Type XXX to end."
jot=0
REPEAT
  jot=jot+1
  PRINT "Jotting number ";jot
  INPUT temp$
  IF temp$<>"XXX" THEN note$(jot)=temp$
UNTIL temp$="XXX" OR jot=100
jot=jot-1
freespace=pointer(jot)
pointer(jot)=-1
active=jot
IF jot=100 THEN PRINT "This Jotter page is full."
RETURN

LABEL editor
REPEAT
  CLS
  PRINT "EDIT MENU"
  PRINT
  PRINT "Display Jottings .........1"
  PRINT "Change a Jotting .........2"
  PRINT "Insert a Jotting .........3"
  PRINT "Delete a Jotting ........4"
  PRINT "Move a Jotting...........5"
  PRINT "Make into a Heading ......6"
  PRINT "Exit from Edit Mode ......7"

  REPEAT
    opt$=INKEY$
  UNTIL opt$>="1" AND opt$<="7"
  opt=VAL(opt$)
  IF opt<7 THEN ON opt GOSUB showfile,change,injot,deletejot,movejot,header
UNTIL opt$="7"
saved=0
RETURN
```

```
LABEL showfile
GOSUB show
GOSUB anykey
RETURN

LABEL show
count=1
shownum=pointer(0)
REPEAT
  PRINT #outwhere,shownum,note$(shownum)
  shownum=pointer(shownum)
  count=count+1
  IF count=20 AND outwhere=1 THEN GOSUB pageful
UNTIL shownum=-1
RETURN

LABEL pageful
PRINT
GOSUB anykey
count=1
RETURN

LABEL change
REPEAT
  CLS
  PRINT "Change a Jotting"
  GOSUB show
  INPUT "Jotting number ";jot
  INPUT "New jotting ";note$(jot)
  INPUT "Change another (Y/N) ";again$
UNTIL UPPER$(again$)="N"
RETURN

LABEL injot
REPEAT
  CLS
  PRINT "Insert AFTER which jotting?"
  GOSUB show
  INPUT "Jotting number ";jot
  empty=freespace
  freespace=pointer(freespace)
  pointer(empty)=pointer(jot)
  pointer(jot)=empty
  jot=empty
  INPUT "Jotting to be inserted ";note$(jot)
  INPUT "Insert another (Y/N) ";again$
```

```
UNTIL UPPER$(again$)="N"
RETURN


LABEL deletejot
REPEAT
  CLS
  PRINT "Delete which jotting?"
  GOSUB show
  INPUT "Jotting number ";jot
  GOSUB findpointer
  pointer(this)=pointer(jot)
  pointer(jot)=freespace
  freespace=jot
  INPUT "Delete another (Y/N) ";again$
UNTIL UPPER$(again$)="N"
RETURN


LABEL movejot
REPEAT
  CLS
  PRINT "Move which jotting?"
  INPUT "Jotting number ";jot
  GOSUB findpointer
  pointer(this)=pointer(jot)
  INPUT "Insert after which Jotting ";after
  pointer(jot)=pointer(after)
  pointer(after)=jot
  INPUT "Move another (Y/N) ";again$
UNTIL UPPER$(again$)="N"
RETURN


LABEL header
CLS
REPEAT
  PRINT "Which jotting becomes a heading?"
  GOSUB show
  INPUT "Jotting number ";jot
  note$(jot)=UPPER$(note$(jot))
  CLS
  GOSUB show
  INPUT "Another heading? (Y/N) ",an$
UNTIL UPPER$(an$)="N"
RETURN


LABEL findpointer
FOR loop=0 TO 100
```

```
   IF pointer(loop)=jot THEN this=loop:loop=101
NEXT loop
RETURN


LABEL printer
outwhere=0
PRINT "Check that printer is ready."
GOSUB anykey
GOSUB show
PRINT #0
RETURN


LABEL lister
CLS
PRINT "File";TAB(10);"No.of notes";TAB(30);"First note begins..."
flag=1
file$=FIND$("*.JOT")
WHILE file$<>""
  OPEN #5 INPUT file$
  INPUT #5,active
  INPUT #5,note$
  PRINT LEFT$(file$,8);TAB(10);active;TAB(30);LEFT$(note$,40)
  CLOSE 5
  flag=flag+1
  file$=FIND$("*.JOT",flag)
WEND
IF flag=1 THEN PRINT "No Jottings on this disk"
GOSUB anykey
RETURN


LABEL loader
GOSUB getfilename
OPEN #5 INPUT filename$
INPUT #5,active
FOR loop=0 TO 100
  pointer(loop)=loop+1
NEXT loop
FOR loop=1 TO active
INPUT #5,note$(loop)
  NEXT loop
CLOSE 5
pointer(active)=-1
freespace=active+1
RETURN
```

```
LABEL saver
PRINT "Saving file ";filename$
OPEN #5 OUTPUT filename$
PRINT #5,active
shownum=pointer(0)
REPEAT
  PRINT #5,note$(shownum)
  shownum=pointer(shownum)
UNTIL shownum=-1
CLOSE 5
saved=1
RETURN

LABEL killer
GOSUB getfilename
KILL filename$
RETURN

LABEL rename
GOSUB getfilename
REPEAT
  INPUT "New file name? ";temp$
  temp$=UPPER$(temp$)+"          "
  temp$=LEFT$(temp$,8)+".JOT"
  file$=FIND$(temp$)
  IF file$=temp$ THEN PRINT "Name already in use."
UNTIL file$<>temp$
NAME filename$ AS temp$
filename$=temp$
RETURN

LABEL getfilename
REPEAT
  INPUT "Name of file ";filename$
  filename$=UPPER$(filename$)+"          "
  filename$=LEFT$(filename$,8)+".JOT"
  file$=FIND$(filename$)
  IF file$<>filename$ THEN PRINT "File not present on disk"
UNTIL file$=filename$
RETURN

LABEL exit
IF saved=0 THEN GOSUB checksave
RETURN
```

```
LABEL checksave
PRINT "Current file has not been saved. Exit (Y/N)"
REPEAT
  a$=UPPER$(INKEY$)
UNTIL a$="Y" OR a$="N"
IF a$="N" THEN GOSUB savepara
RETURN

LABEL anykey
PRINT "Press any key to go on."
REPEAT
  a$=INKEY$
UNTIL a$<>""
RETURN
```

Chapter 7

The Self-taught Computer

When you first start to play noughts and crosses against this program you might be inclined to say to yourself, 'Artificial intelligence? This looks more like genuine stupidity!' But give it a chance — it gets better. After a while it will start to give you a run for your money, and it will eventually reach a stage where it can almost always force a draw and occasionally manage a win.

Noughts and crosses is a trivial game, but its simplicity allows us to concentrate on the principles and techniques of analysing situations and developing routines that enable the computer to make educated and rational decisions. It is feasible to analyse noughts and crosses completely and to write routines that will ensure that the computer always makes the best possible move. This has not been done in our program — OXO — though we will come back to it later to see how it can be managed. Instead, I have approached the game as if it was one where all the alternative situations could not been known in advance. This approach could well be employed profitably in more complex games and in simulations of real world activities.

In essence, all the computer is told is what constitutes a win. It then records every game that is played and when deciding a move it reviews all past games in search of comparable situations. Every time it finds one where the previous moves have been the same as in the current game, it makes a note of the next move and of who won; when all games have been checked, it assesses the possible 'next moves' to see which would be most likely to produce a favourable result.

For example, with 500 or so past games in store, and the current game on its sixth move, the computer finds itself in the situation shown in Figure 7.1.

In checking the past games, it finds 20 that had followed through the same sequence of

O	X	O
d	X	f
X	h	i

FIGURE 7.1

moves to get to this point. It then evaluates the next moves on whether the game resulted in a loss, win or draw. (Note that for simplicity a draw is counted as good as a win.) The possible next moves can be summarised:

Next move?	Past results	Move value
d	3 Lost, 0 Won/Drawn	-3
f	3 Lost, 2 Won/Drawn	-1
h	2 Lost, 6 Won/Drawn	+4
i	3 Lost, 1 Won/Drawn	-2

On this basis, the best move is into box 'h', at the centre bottom; and indeed, this is the move that most people would make here. When the computer has only a limited set of past games to work on, its moves are not so rational and it loses regularly. But at least it learns from its mistakes!

When you run OXO, you will see that it has 'Game' and 'Learn' modes. This is slightly ambiguous as it plays and learns in both modes; the difference is that in 'Learn' mode it plays against itself, rather than against an opponent on the other side of the keyboard. In practice, it learns much quicker if it can play against a good player because it will record his, or her, moves and copy successful sequences in subsequent games. If it learns only by playing against itself, it is still a pretty indifferent player after several hundred games. (There are 362,880 different ways in which you can arrange nine symbols. Even after you have discounted those that lead to a win before the ninth move, there are still many thousands of ways of playing the game.)

Intelligence by analysis

No matter how many moves there may be in theory, we all know that in practice there are only a very limited number of worthwhile moves at any stage of the game. In that last example, the player must take the bottom centre box to prevent his opponent from winning on the next go.

At any point in the game, this set of action rules will normally produce the best move:

FILES AND DIRECTORIES

1   If you have two in a line, complete the line to win.

2   If the opponent has two in a line, take the last box and block him.

3   If a line has one of yours, consider it.

4   If a box is at the junction of two lines, each containing one of yours, then take it. This guarantees a win next go.

5   If a line has one of each, don't use it.

6   If there is no definite move to make, take the first box that gives you access to most lines — discounting those that cannot be used. The centre is usually the best as this can access up to four lines. Corners are next best as they can access up to three each.

The same set can be used even at the beginning of the game, although at that stage only rule 6 will apply. To give variety in the screen appearance of the game — though not in its actual playing, rule 6 could be changed so that where there are several equally good moves, the computer picks one at random instead of taking the first. (If your opponent has taken the centre on the first move, it doesn't matter which corner you take as long as you do take one.)

This set of rules can be implemented in several ways. The method described below is convenient and fits in with the structure of the OXO program.
In OXO, the playing area is mapped in the string array *grid$* (see Figure 7.2). This is initialised to hold the letters a to i, which are used both for identifying the boxes on the screen and for recording the game sequence in the *move$* variable. Thus, after the moves, Centre, Top Left, Bottom Centre, *move$* would hold *eah*.

	0	1	2
0	a	b	c
1	d	e	f
2	g	h	i

FIGURE 7.2

The alternative next moves are evaluated in a one-dimensional number array *possible*. The conversion from two to one dimensions is done by the formula:

82

possible place = gridrow*3 + gridcolumn

For example, box 'f' is mapped by *possible(5)* − 3*1 + 2. There is also a simple conversion between grid letters and *possible* numbers:

possible place = ASC(letter) − 97
grid letter = CHR$(possible place + 97)

In the existing 'experiential learning' system, moves are evaluated in the following way. Where the move led on to a won or drawn game, the associated *possible* element is incremented by 1; where the game is lost, the value in *possible* is reduced by 1. After all past games have been reviewed, the best move will be that which has the higher *possible* value. We can use the same array in this approach to the computer's play.

The grid has eight lines that must be assessed − three horizontal, three vertical and two diagonal. There are 27 possible combinations of X, O and space in any line, but if position is ignored, this can be reduced to 10. (For example, X − −, − X − and − − X are all equivalent.) If we count Os as worth 1 and Xs as 4, we can get a simple number for checking (see Table 7.1). For the purposes of this example we will assume that the computer is playing 'O'; in practice, the program can be made flexible so that it can play either side.

TABLE 7.1

Grid line	Number equivalent	Check total	Possible value	
- - -	0 0 0	0	Usable	1
O - -	1 0 0	1	Worthwhile	2
O O -	1 1 0	2	Must do!!	99
O O O	1 1 1	3	Game over	N/A
X - -	4 0 0	4	Ignore	0
X O -	4 1 0	5	Ignore	0
X O O	4 1 1	6	Ignore	0
X X -	4 4 0	8	Block it!	9
X X O	4 4 1	9	Ignore	0
X X X	4 4 4	12	Game over	N/A

There are only four check totals that require any action. A line total of 0 or 1 means that the empty boxes are worth considering if there are no more pressing demands, and a 0 line is less valuable than a 1 line. The *possible* elements that map those boxes should be incremented by 1 or 2, respectively. A box at the junction of two good lines

83

File   Program   Edit   Fonts   Colours   Patterns   Lines   Windows   BASIC2

```
H |    Results-2                              ◊%◊
Game or Learn Mode (
G/L) ?g
Your move ?e
Your move ?g
Your move ?c
You win
Total Games Recorded
 1
Same Games  0
Another Game ?y
Your move ?a
Your move ?c
Your move ?h
Your move ?f
Draw
Total Games Recorded
 2
Same Games  0
Another Game ?y
Your move ?e
Your move ?g
Your move ?
```

would therefore finish up with a value of 4. If the line's check total is 2, then the empty box must be taken, and this can be reflected in an extremely high *possible* value. Finally, if it is 8, then the empty box should be taken − as long as there is no possible winning line − and the *possible* value here should reflect the priority.

This Basic2 routine will handle the checks and evaluations for the horizontal lines. The vertical and diagonal lines can be handled through two similar loops:

```
FOR gr=0 TO 2
check=0:e1=-1:e2=-1
FOR gc=0 TO 2
IF grid$(gr,gc)='X' THEN check=check+1:GOTO nextcol
IF grid$(gr,gc)='O' THEN check=check+4:GOTO nextcol
IF e1=-1 THEN e1=gr*3+gc ELSE e2=gr*3+gc
LABEL nextcol
NEXT gc
IF check=0 THEN FOR gc=0 TO 2:possible(gr*3+gc)=possible(gr*3+gc)+1:NEXT gc
IF check=1 THEN possible(e1)=possible(e1)+2:possible(e2)=possible(e2)+2
IF check=2 THEN possible(e1)=99
IF check=8 THEN possible(e1)=9
NEXT gr
```

e1 and *e2* will record the empty boxes, if any. Structured programming enthusiasts who eschew the use of GOTOs can replace the set of lines in the *gc* loop with a single line of nested IFs:

```
IF grid$(gr,gc)='X' THEN check=check+1 ELSE IF grid$(gr,gc)='0' THEN
check=check+4 ELSE IF e1=-1 THEN e1=gr*3+gc ELSE e2=gr*3+gc
```

Program structure

Initialisation

    Initialise screen
      Window 1, graphics
      Window 2, text

    Initialise arrays and load old gamefile if present

Game mode

Game mode	
Repeat	
Set up frame	*drawframe*
Play game	*gameplay*
Repeat	
First player either you or me	
If you, then ask for move	*you*
if me, then find best move	*me/lookback*
Check for win or end	*check*
Second player either me or you	*me/lookback/you*
Check for win or end	*check*
Until game over	
Record game sequence	*checkfile*
Swap so other player starts next time	
Until no more games wanted	

Learn mode

Learn mode	*learn*
Play 500 games (or however many you want)	
Repeat	
Make me play 'X' and find move	*me/lookback*

Check for win or end	*check*
Make me play 'O' and find move	*me/lookback*
Check for win or end	*check*
Until game over	
Record game sequence	*checkfile*
Save game file	*closedown*
Move finding subroutine	*lookback*
Compare move sequence with past games	
If the same to that point, note next move	
increment possible if won or drawn	
decrement possible if game lost	
Check through possibles for highest value	

The OXO program

```
REM oxo

 REM initialise
SCREEN #1 GRAPHICS 480 FIXED,200 FIXED
USER #1, SPACE 480,200
WINDOW #1 FULL ON
WINDOW #1 PLACE 160,200

SCREEN #2 TEXT 20 FIXED,22 FIXED
WINDOW #2 PLACE 0,0
WINDOW #2 FULL ON
WINDOW #2 OPEN
youstart=0

DRIVE "B"
 REM please yourself which drive
DIM old$(500)
DIM grid$(2,2),x(2,2),y(2,2)
DIM possible(8)
x$=FIND$("MOVES.OXO")
IF x$<>"MOVES    .OXO" THEN num=0:GOTO begin
PRINT #2,"Loading old games"
OPEN #5 INPUT x$
INPUT #5,numgames
FOR game=1 TO numgames
  INPUT #5,old$(game)
NEXT game
CLOSE #5
```

```
LABEL begin
youstart=1:my$="o":your$="x"
INPUT #2,"Game or Learn Mode (G/L) ";a$
IF UPPER$(a$)="L" THEN GOTO learn

 REM game mode main loop
REPEAT
  GOSUB drawframe
  GOSUB gameplay
  INPUT #2,"Another Game ";a$
  a$=UPPER$(a$)
UNTIL a$<>"Y"
GOSUB closedown
END


LABEL learn
samenum=0
 REM Warning! 500 games take a few hours to play!
FOR game=1 TO 500
  GOSUB drawframe
  win=0
  move$=""
  REPEAT
    which$="x"
    my$="x":your$="o":GOSUB me
    GOSUB check
    IF win<>0 THEN GOTO exit
    my$="o":your$="x":GOSUB me
    GOSUB check
    LABEL exit
  UNTIL win<>0
  GOSUB checkfile
NEXT game
GOSUB closedown
END


LABEL gameplay
win=0
move$=""
REPEAT
  which$="x"
  IF youstart THEN GOSUB you ELSE GOSUB me
  GOSUB check
  IF win<>0 THEN GOTO exitgame
  IF youstart THEN GOSUB me ELSE GOSUB you
  GOSUB check
```

```
    LABEL exitgame
UNTIL win<>0
GOSUB checkfile
SWAP my$,your$
IF youstart=1 THEN youstart=0 ELSE youstart=1
RETURN


LABEL checkfile
same=0
FOR game=1 TO numgames
   IF old$(game)=move$ THEN same=1:game=numgames
NEXT game
IF same THEN samenum=samenum+1
numgames=numgames+1
old$(numgames)=move$
 REM it can be worth recording identical games
PRINT #2,"Total Games Recorded ";numgames
PRINT #2,"Same Games ";samenum
RETURN


LABEL drawframe
RESTORE drawframe
FOR grow=0 TO 2
  FOR col=0 TO 2
    READ grid$(grow,col),x(grow,col),y(grow,col)
  NEXT col
NEXT grow
REM identifying letters and symbol co-ordinates
DATA a,120,140,b,200,140,c,280,140
DATA d,120,100,e,200,100,f,280,100
DATA g,120,60,h,200,60,i,280,60

CLS #1
LINE 80;120,320;120 WIDTH 5
LINE 80;80,320;80 WIDTH 5
LINE 160;40,160;160 WIDTH 5
LINE 240;40,240;160 WIDTH 5
FOR grow=0 TO 2
  FOR col=0 TO 2
    MOVE x(grow,col);y(grow,col)
    PRINT FONT(2) POINTS(18) grid$(grow,col)
  NEXT col
NEXT grow
RETURN
```

```
LABEL me
mymove=0
GOSUB lookback
IF mymove=0 THEN GOSUB random_move
GOSUB mark
RETURN

LABEL lookback
FOR mygo=0 TO 8:possible(mygo)=0:NEXT mygo

FOR oldgo=1 TO numgames
  this$=old$(oldgo)
  same=1:count=0
  WHILE count<LEN(move$) AND same=1
    count=count+1
    IF MID$(move$,count,1)<>MID$(this$,count,1) THEN same=0
  WEND
  IF same=0 THEN GOTO nextold
  nextmove$=MID$(this$,count+1,1)
  mygo=ASC(nextmove$)-97
  IF RIGHT$(this$,1)=my$ THEN possible(mygo)=possible(mygo)+1 ELSE
       IF RIGHT$(this$,1)=your$ THEN possible(mygo)=possible(mygo)-1

  LABEL nextold
NEXT oldgo
high=-99:best=0
FOR mygo=0 TO 8
  grow=mygo\3:col=mygo MOD 3:ingrid$=grid$(grow,col)
  IF ingrid$="x" OR ingrid$="o"THEN GOTO nextposs
  IF possible(mygo)>high THEN high=possible(mygo):best=mygo
  LABEL nextposs
NEXT mygo
grow=best\3:col=best MOD 3:mymove=1
RETURN

 REM not used in this version
LABEL random_move
REPEAT
  try=0
  REPEAT
    grow=RND(3)-1
    col=RND(3)-1
    mygo=grow*3+col
    try=try+1
  UNTIL possible(mygo)=0 OR try>5
UNTIL grid$(grow,col)>="a" AND grid$(grow,col)<="i"
RETURN
```

```
LABEL you
REPEAT
  movenum=0
  WHILE movenum=0
    INPUT #2,"Your move ";a$
    movenum=INSTR("abcdefghi",LOWER$(a$))
  WEND
  movenum=movenum-1
  grow=movenum\3
  col=movenum MOD 3
UNTIL grid$(grow,col))>="a" AND grid$(grow,col)<="i"
GOSUB mark
RETURN


LABEL mark
move$=move$+grid$(grow,col)
grid$(grow,col)=which$
x=x(grow,col):y=y(grow,col)
MOVE x;y:PRINT POINTS(16);" "
IF which$="x" THEN LINE x-20;y-10,x+20;y+10 WIDTH 5:
- LINE x-20;y+10,x+20;y-10 WIDTH 5
IF which$="o" THEN ELLIPSE x;y,30,0.5 WIDTH 5
IF which$="x" THEN which$="o" ELSE which$="x"
RETURN


LABEL check
FOR grow=0 TO 2
IF grid$(grow,0)=grid$(grow,1) AND grid$(grow,0)=grid$(grow,2) THEN
 - win$=grid$(grow,0):GOSUB winner:grow=2
NEXT grow
FOR col=0 TO 2
IF grid$(0,col)=grid$(1,col) AND grid$(0,col)=grid$(2,col) THEN
 - win$=grid$(0,col):GOSUB winner:col=2
NEXT col
IF grid$(0,0)=grid$(1,1) AND grid$(0,0)=grid$(2,2) THEN
 - win$=grid$(0,0):GOSUB winner
IF grid$(0,2)=grid$(1,1) AND grid$(0,2)=grid$(2,0) THEN
 - win$=grid$(0,2):GOSUB winner
IF win=0 AND LEN(move$)=9 THEN win$="d":GOSUB winner
RETURN


LABEL winner
IF win$=your$ THEN PRINT #2;"You win" ELSE IF win$=my$ THEN
  PRINT #2;"I win" ELSE PRINT #2,"Draw"
win=1
IF win$="d" THEN win$="o"
```

```
 REM draw counts as victory for second player
move$=move$+win$
RETURN

LABEL closedown
OPEN #5 OUTPUT "MOVES.OXO"
PRINT #5,numgames
FOR game=1 TO numgames
  PRINT #5,old$(game)
NEXT game
CLOSE #5
RETURN
```

PART 3

GRAPHICS AND
SCREEN DISPLAYS

Chapter 8

Frame Design and Costing

As it stands, this program may prove of use to someone in the picture-framing business or to DIY framers; with some fairly straightforward alterations it could also be used for costing replacement windows or double glazing. On a more general note, it is intended to demonstrate that graphics can be integrated with calculations so that design and costing can be performed as a single operation.

To use the program, you must first give details of the types of glass and framing that may be used. All that is needed for the glass is its identifying name and cost per square metre. For the frame you will need to give a name, widths and cost per metre. Two width measurements are needed for each frame type (see Figure 8.1). Width A is of the inside lip of the frame where the picture and glass will fit; width B refers to the remainder. Only width A is relevant when calculating the glass size; the full width is needed for the overall size of the framed picture and the cost of the framing material.

FIGURE 8.1

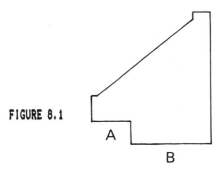

When a frame is being designed, the picture size and frame type is specified. From this, the program will produce a sample scale diagram. While this will not show the colours of picture, frame and border, the diagram will at least give a very good idea of the proportions of the finished object.

Initially, the depth of the border around the picture is set at one eight of the picture width. This can be altered by using the cursor keys — and note that the horizontal and vertical borders can be adjusted independently. If a different style of frame is wanted, this can be done at this stage.

Each time the diagram is redrawn, the program will recalculate and display the costs of glass, frame, border card and backing material.

Program structure

Initialisation

    Initialise screen — single graphics window
    Initialise arrays and load files

Main loop

    Display menu — with 'picture frame' outline
    Perform options
    Until exit
    On exit, save files if updated

Options

    Glass types and prices
      Display existing file
      Repeat
        Take in details of additional types
      Until no more new types
      Set fileflag to show file needs saving

    Frame types
      Display existing file
      Draw generalised frame cross-section
      Repeat
        Take in details of additional types
      Until no more new types
      Set fileflag

Design and costing
 Get key details — picture size, frame type, glass type
 Repeat
  Display scale diagram
  Display costs
  Get key press
   Cursors change frame size — recalculate
   'Home' selects new frame type — recalculate
 Until 'End' pressed

Key subroutines

Calculate
 Scale picture to screen size
 Work out inner and outer dimensions for frame —
  picture + border + frame widths
 Scale frame dimensions to screen size
 If outer frame too large for screen, adjust scale and start again
 Calculate glass, border card, backing and frame sizes and costs

Oops
 Open Window 2, Text
 Display error message
 Wait for ESCape press before closing

Notes

Scaling

The aim here is to make maximum use of the screen display — to draw the frame diagram as large as possible. With the graphics screen defined as 640 by 200, each pixel is twice as high as it is wide. Bearing this in mind, only a single scale is used but the resulting y values are divided by two before drawing. Overall, the screen area used by the diagram is 480 pixels wide by 200 high so there is effectively a width-to-height ratio of 1:1.2.

The scale is initially set to half the width or half the height of the picture, depending upon its shape. The line is:

```
scale=240/wide:IF high/wide>1.2 THEN scale=200/high
```

During the design routine, the scale will be reduced if adjustments to the border size or frame type have expanded the diagram beyond the screen limits. This will only be known part way through the *calculate* routine, hence the line:

```
IF picoutwidth>480 or picoutheight>200 THEN scale=scale*0.9:GOTO calculate
```

As there are over 20 variables holding the dimensions of the picture, frame and diagram, Table 8.1 may be of help!

TABLE 8.1

Variables	Data
fwa	Inside lip of framing wood/metal
fwb	Outside ledge of framing
wide	
high	Actual picture size
innerwidth	
innerheight	Inside of actual frame = wide + border
outerwidth	
outerheight	Outside of actual frame = innerheight + 2*(fwa+fwb)
picwidth	
picheight	Scaled picture size
picinwidth	
picinheight	Scaled inside frame
picoutwidth	
picoutheight	Scaled outside frame
x,y	Bottom left corner of picture
xin,yin	Bottom left of inside of frame
xout,yout	Bottom left of outside of frame
glasswidth	
glassheight	Actual glass size

The Oops window

In this program, error messages — displayed when trying to use an undefined type of glass or frame — are handled through a second window. It is opened specially for the occasion and closed again once the user has got the message.

The Basic2 window-handling commands are comprehensive and quite straightforward to use; but where windows are needed on an open-and-shut basis — as for error messages or menus — the limitations of the system soon become obvious. When a window is closed, the whole window beneath is redrawn. And it is *redrawn*, not simply copied out from screen memory. On a graphics screen, the system retains a list of the most recent graphics commands and works through this list to recreate the lower window. This is in contrast to the proper GEM system, where the lower window is refreshed instantly from memory when a foreground window is closed.

In this particular program, the redrawing is rarely more than an irritating flicker — though data may be lost from the design screen if there has been a long series of adjustments; but in the transformations program (Chapter 10) where the screen may contain complex graphics, the redrawing takes an appreciable time and may not fully restore the screen display.

Despite the limitations, pop-up windows can add a certain something to screen displays. Retain the Oops window if you like it; if not reserve a small section of the screen — top or bottom line, or a corner — for your error messages and display them there.

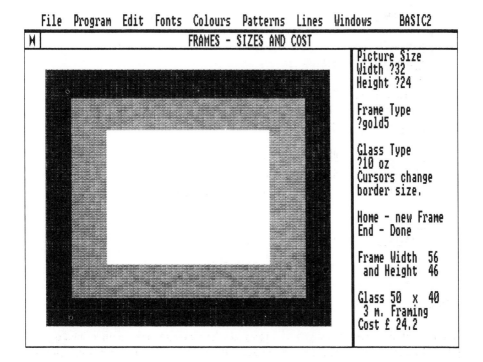

Framing program

```
REM framing

SCREEN #1 GRAPHICS 640 FIXED,200 FIXED
USER #1 SPACE 640,200
WINDOW #1,TITLE "FRAMES - SIZES AND COST"
WINDOW #1 FULL ON

DIM glass$(10),glass(10)
  REM 10 types, and prices
DIM frame$(20),frame(20,3)
  REM 20 types, width, internal width & price
DRIVE "B"
fileflag=0
numg=0:numf=0
  REM number of Glass & Frame types
x$=FIND$("framing.dat"):IF x$="" THEN GOTO main
OPEN #5 INPUT "FRAMING.DAT"
INPUT #5,numg
FOR types=1 TO numg
  INPUT #5,glass$(types)
  INPUT #5,glass(types)
NEXT types
IF EOF(#5) THEN CLOSE #5:GOTO main
INPUT #5,numf
FOR types=1 TO numf
  INPUT #5,frame$(types)
  INPUT #5,frame(types,1),frame(types,2),frame(types,3)
NEXT types
CLOSE #5

cardage=1.50
  REM £ 1.50 per sq.m. charge for border card
backing=2
  REM £ 2.00 per sq.m. charge for backing

LABEL main
REPEAT
  CLS
  BOX 32;10,576,180 COLOUR 14 FILL
  BOX 72;30,496,140 COLOUR 5 FILL
  BOX 128;50,384,100 COLOUR 0 FILL

  PRINT AT (22;8);"Glass Types and Prices.............1"
  PRINT AT (22;10);"Frame Types and Prices.............2"
```

```
    PRINT AT (22;12);"Frame Design and Costing..........3"
    PRINT AT (22;14);"Exit from Program.................4"

    opt$=INKEY$
    WHILE opt$<"1" OR opt$>"4"
      opt$=INKEY$
    WEND

    opt=VAL(opt$):ON opt GOSUB glasstypes,frametypes,costing,exit

UNTIL opt=4
END

LABEL glasstypes
CLS
PRINT "XXX to End"
PRINT
PRINT TAB(10);"Description";TAB(30);"Price per square metre"
FOR types=1 TO numg
  PRINT TAB(10);glass$(types);TAB(30);glass(types)
NEXT types
REPEAT
  numg=numg+1
  PRINT TAB(10);:INPUT glass$(numg);
  IF glass$(numg)<>"XXX" THEN PRINT TAB(30);:INPUT glass(numg)
UNTIL glass$(numg)="XXX"
numg=numg-1
fileflag=1

RETURN

LABEL frametypes
CLS
PRINT "XXX to End                  Widths in centimetres"
PRINT
PRINT TAB(10);"Description";TAB(30);"Width A";TAB(40);"Width B";
-   TAB(50);"Price per metre"
FOR types=1 TO numf
  PRINT TAB(10);frame$(types);TAB(30);frame(types,1);TAB(40);
  - frame(types,2);TAB(50);frame(types,3)
NEXT types
SHAPE 540;175,540;180,620;190,620;160,570;160,570;175,540;175
LINE 540;170,570;170 START 1 END 1
MOVE 550;166:PRINT "A"
LINE 570;150,620;150 START 1 END 1
MOVE 590;146:PRINT "B"
```

```
numf=numf+1
INPUT AT(10;numf+4);frame$(numf);
WHILE frame$(numf)<>"XXX"
  INPUT AT(30;numf+4);frame(numf,1);
  INPUT AT(40;numf+4);frame(numf,2);
  INPUT AT(50;numf+4);frame(numf,3)
  numf=numf+1
  INPUT AT(10;numf+4);frame$(numf);
WEND
 REM a REPEAT...UNTIL loop could have been used here as in glasstypes
 REM but the WHILE...WEND is more convenient with several INPUTs
numf=numf-1
fileflag=1
RETURN

LABEL costing
CLS
IF numf*numg=0 THEN message$="Glass/Frames not defined":GOSUB oops:RETURN
LINE 480;0,480;200 WIDTH 7
PRINT AT (62;1);"Picture Size"
INPUT AT (62;2);"Width ";wide
INPUT AT (62;3);"Height ";high
scale=240/wide:IF high/wide>1.2 THEN scale=200/high
side=INT(wide/4):top=side
PRINT AT (62;5);"Frame Type "
GOSUB frameselect
PRINT AT (62;8);"Glass Type"

REPEAT
  PRINT AT(62;9);"                 "
  INPUT AT(62;9);gtype$
  gtype=0
  FOR types=1 TO numg
    IF gtype$=glass$(types) THEN gtype=types
  NEXT types
  IF gtype=0 THEN message$="Type Unknown":GOSUB oops
UNTIL gtype>0

PRINT AT (62;10);"Cursors change"
PRINT AT (62;11);"border size."
PRINT AT (62;13);"Home - new Frame"
PRINT AT (62;14);"End - Done"
PRINT AT (62;16);"Frame Width "
PRINT AT (62;17);" and Height "
GOSUB calculate
```

```
REPEAT
  a=-1
  WHILE a=-1
    a=INKEY
  WEND
  IF a=328 THEN top=top+2
    REM up arrow widens top and bottom borders
  IF a=336 AND top>0 THEN top=top-2
    REM down arrow shrinks same
  IF a=331 THEN side=side+2
    REM left arrow widens side borders
  IF a=333 AND side>0 THEN side=side-2
    REM right arrow shrinks these
  IF a=327 THEN GOSUB frameselect:GOSUB calculate
    REM home for new frame
  IF a<>335 AND a<>327 THEN GOSUB calculate
UNTIL a=335
  REM end key
PRINT AT(2;21);"Press any key to return to main menu"
a$=""
WHILE a$=""
  a$=INKEY$
WEND

RETURN

LABEL frameselect
REPEAT
  PRINT AT(62;6);"                "
  INPUT AT(62;6);fr$
  ftype=0
  FOR types=1 TO numf
    IF fr$=frame$(types) THEN ftype=types
  NEXT types
  IF ftype=0 THEN message$="Type Unknown!":GOSUB oops
UNTIL ftype>0
fwa=frame(ftype,1):fwb=frame(ftype,2)
framewidth=fwa+fwb
RETURN

LABEL calculate
picwidth=wide*scale
picheight=high*scale/2
x=240-picwidth/2
y=100-picheight/2
innerwidth=wide+side
```

```
   REM side borders initially set to quarter of picture width in total
innerheight=high+top
   REM top and bottom borders initially the same as side borders
outerwidth=innerwidth+framewidth*2
outerheight=innerheight+framewidth*2
picinwidth=innerwidth*scale
picinheight=innerheight*scale/2
picoutwidth=outerwidth*scale
picoutheight=outerheight*scale/2
xin=240-picinwidth/2
yin=100-picinheight/2
xout=240-picoutwidth/2
yout=100-picoutheight/2
IF picoutwidth>480 OR picoutheight>200 THEN scale=scale*0.9:GOTO calculate
PRINT AT (74;16);outerwidth
PRINT AT (74;17);outerheight
glasswidth=innerwidth+2*fwa
glassheight=innerheight+2*fwa
PRINT AT (62;19);"Glass";glasswidth;" x ";glass_height
framelength=((outerwidth+outerheight)*2)/100
framelength=INT(framelength)+1
   REM round up to next full metre
PRINT AT (62;20);framelength;"m. Framing"
glassarea=(glasswidth*glassheight)/1000
   REM sizes in cms., prices in square metres
glasscost=glassarea*glass(gtype)
framecost=framelength*frame(ftype,3)
cardcost=glassarea*cardage
IF side+top=0 THEN cardcost=0
 REM no border card used
backcost=glassarea*backing
cost=glasscost+framecost+cardcost+backing
PRINT AT (62;21);"Cost £";ROUND(cost,2)

LABEL boxer
BOX 0;0,480,200 COLOUR 0 FILL
BOX xout;yout,picoutwidth,picoutheight COLOUR 14 FILL
BOX xin;yin,picinwidth,picinheight COLOUR 5 FILL
BOX x;y,picwidth,picheight COLOUR 0 FILL
RETURN

LABEL oops
WINDOW #2 CLOSE
SCREEN #2 TEXT 30 FIXED,5 FIXED
WINDOW #2,TITLE "OOPS"
WINDOW #2,PLACE 180;60
```

```
WINDOW #2 OPEN
PRINT #2, AT(2;2);message$
PRINT #2, AT(2;4);"Press ESCAPE to Continue"
WHILE INKEY<>27:WEND
WINDOW #2 CLOSE
RETURN

LABEL exit
IF fileflag=0 THEN RETURN
OPEN #5 OUTPUT "FRAMING.DAT"
PRINT #5,numg
FOR types=1 TO numg
  PRINT #5,glass$(types)
  PRINT #5,glass(types)
NEXT types
PRINT #5,numf
FOR types=1 TO numf
  PRINT #5,frame$(types)
  PRINT #5,frame(types,1),frame(types,2),frame(types,3)
NEXT types
CLOSE #5
RETURN
```

Chapter 9

Seat Plans and Bookings

Organising a coach trip? In charge of the tickets for an amateur dramatic production? Planning the seating arrangements for a big do? This program, either as it stands or with only minor modifications, can help to simplify the organisation.

The seating plan is created in two stages. First the maximum number of rows and columns is entered − and remember that a typical coach will have five or six seats across the back row, but elsewhere only four across. From this, the program produces a basic grid. The unwanted 'seats' − the centre aisle and the areas around the doors and driver − are then removed by clicking them with the mouse button. Seats removed in error can be replaced by clicking that part of the grid a second time. When the layout is correct, codes are written onto the seats to identify them. These codes follow the reality of the seating plan, rather than simply being grid references. Thus, the back row may be coded A1 to A5, but the next row − with only four seats − would have the codes B1 to B4.

In the updating routine, a seat can be marked as empty, reserved or paid for. Colour coding is used for easy identification of status − red equals empty, green is reserved, blue is paid for. To change a seat's status, click on it, then select from the menu that will appear at the top of the screen. When a seat is reserved, the program will ask for the person's name. When the seat is paid for, the reserved name − if any − will be shown and can be changed if necessary. The program will then produce a simple ticket showing the tour name, description and seat code.

A totals routine is there so that you can get a quick summary of how the bookings are going; and the Seating List option will give a full printout of the seat reservations.

Program structure

Initialisation

    Initialise window
    Initialise arrays

Main loop

Main loop	*begin*
Repeat	
Display menu	
Perform options	
Until exit	
On exit, save file if updated	*exit*

Options

Layout Coach Seating	*layout*
Get number of rows and columns	
Scale and draw basic grid of seats	
Print instructions	
Repeat (check mouse and button when clicked..)	
If on seat then remove/replace seat	*getseat*
If on 'Seat Codes', write codes in	*seatcodes*
If on 'Done' box, exit	
Until done	
Get trip name, description and seat price	*getname*
Set update flag for file saving	
Seat bookings	*book*
Use current coach or load new?	*oldtour/gettour*
Draw grid and seats − colour = status	
Print instructions	
Repeat (check mouse and button when clicked...)	
If on seat then get new status	*updateseat*
Empty, reserved, paid	*reserve/pay*
If paid, then print ticket	
If on 'Done' box, exit	
Until done	
Set file flag for saving	
Show totals	*total*
Current coach or another?	*oldtour/gettour*

Scan seat array to find:
    number of seats empty, reserved, paid for
    total income, total seats available

Current seating list   *list*
   Current coach or another?   *oldtour/gettour*
   Get output direction, paper or screen   *checkprint*
   For every seat print:
      Status, person's name if not empty, paid or not

Key subroutines

Getseat
   Calculate seat row and column from mouse x,y
   Change colour code
      Red to white to remove set from plan
      White to red to replace

Seatcodes
   First row code = "A"
   For all rows
     First column code = "1"
   For all columns
     Where seat is present
       Fix code in seat array
       Write on screen
       Store position and colour
       Next column code
     Adjust code for next row

Gettour
   Get tour filename   *getname*
     If not found, display all files on disk
   Load in file, restructuring compacted data

Notes

Layout

In theory, there is no limit to the number of seats that you may have on a plan — so the system could be used for theatre as well as coach bookings. However, in practice, once you had more than 40 or 50 rows, or more than a dozen seats in a row, the screen display would become so cramped as to be unreadable. For large-scale bookings,

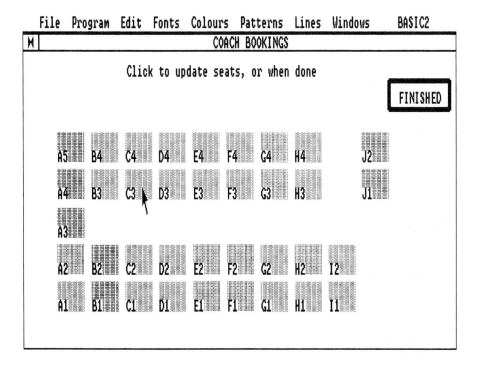

therefore, you would either have to split the plan up into sections or rewrite the program so that it displayed only part of the 'theatre' at a time.

Given the number of rows and columns − and note that the program displays the plan across the screen so that a 'row' of seats appears as a vertical line − the *layout* routine calculates the dimensions for the grid on screen. The maximum *gridx* value is set to 50 as short, but fat, coaches would otherwise make a mess of the overall screen display:

```
gridx=INT(600/(rows+2))
IF gridx>50 THEN gridx=50
endx=gridx*(rows+1)
gridy=gridx/2:endy=gridy*(cross+1)
```

In order to display the seats as smaller boxes within the grid, their dimensions are set at 80% of the grid sizes, and an offset factor will lift their bottom left corners off the grid lines:

```
seatx=gridx*.8:seaty=gridy*.8
xdiff=(gridx-seatx)/2
ydiff=(gridy-seaty)/2
```

The seats are displayed by a nested (columns in rows) loop:

```
BOX gridx*r+xdiff;gridy*c+ydiff,seatx,seaty COLOUR 2 FILL
```

Seat codes

This presented an interesting little problem − how to produce the sequence of strings "A1", "A2",..., and to ensure that the codes matched only the seats, not just every space on the grid. The answer was to use the ASCII codes. You can convert "A" to "B" by taking its ASCII code, adding one, then finding the character referenced by the new code. Thus:

```
nextletter$ = CHR$(ASC(thisletter$)+1)
```

Digits can be sequenced in the same way, though it is worth noting that this only works up to 9. An alternative method would be to retain the current number code in a number variable and use the STR$() function to turn it into a string. The catch here is that the number will have a leading space that will need to be trimmed off unless you are happy to have ticket codes that read "A 1".

A simplified version of the seat coding routine is reproduced here. The actual routine is made more complex by the presence of lines that print the codes on screen and handle the *seat* array in which positions and colours are stored:

```
row$="A"
seatnumber=0
FOR r=1 TO rows
    cross$="1"
    FOR c=1 TO cross
        IF coach(r,c)=0 THEN GOTO nextc
        seatnumber=seatnumber+1
        seat$(seatnumber,1)=row$+cross$
        cross$=CHR$(ASC(cross$)+1)
        LABEL nextc
    NEXT c
    row$=CHR$(ASC(row$)+1)
NEXT r
```

The disk file

The file for each coach needs to store the seat and grid dimensions and the number of seats. Then, for each seat, it must hold the code, reservation name, row, column and colour values. In a sequential file structure it can take quite a lot of disk space to store this information in its raw form. So for disk economy — and as a demonstration of file compaction — the data on each seat is packed into a single string by this set of lines:

```
FOR s=1 TO seatnumber
   rec$=seat$(s,1)+seat$(s,2)
   rec$=rec$+"/"+STR$(seat(s,1))+"/"+STR$(seat(s,2))+STR$(seat(s,3))
      PRINT #5,rec$
NEXT s
```

The record for "B1", reserved for Mrs Brown, would look like this:

"B3Mrs Brown/ 2/ 1 3"

Compacting the data was simple enough, but what about extracting the relevant bits from the string when the file is reloaded?

The seat code is simple enough. It will always be the first two characters of the string, and can be sliced off with LEFT$. MID$ can then be used to remove the rest of the string — note that if you do not specify how many letters to slice the MID$ function takes all the characters to the right of the given number:

```
seat$(s,1)=LEFT$(rec$,2)
rec$=MID$(rec$,3)          (= "2/ 1  3")
```

The end of the reserved name was marked by a "/" during compaction. By hunting for this, we can find the end of the name and slice that off:

```
slash=INSTR(rec$,"/")
seat$(s,2)=LEFT$(rec$,slash-1)
rec$=MID$(rec$,slash+1)          (= " 2/ 1  3")
```

Numbers are a little more complicated. Here also, the slash is used as a divider (isn't it always?), but we must evaluate the string as it is sliced off:

```
slash=INSTR(rec$,"/")
seat(s,1)=VAL(LEFT$(rec$,slash-1))
rec$=MID$(rec$,slash+2)          (= " 1  3")
```

The last two values can now be sliced off to left and right:

```
seat(s,2)=VAL(LEFT$(rec$,LEN(rec$)-1))
seat(s,3)=VAL(RIGHT$(rec$,1))
```

The coach seating program

```
REM coaches

DRIVE "B"

SCREEN #1 GRAPHICS 640 FIXED,200 FIXED
USER #1 SPACE 640,200
WINDOW #1 TITLE "COACH BOOKINGS"
WINDOW #1 FULL ON
fileflag=0
DIM seat$(200,2),seat(200,3) UBYTE
DIM coach(25,8)UBYTE:REM maximum coach 25 x 8

LABEL begin
REPEAT
  CLS
  PRINT AT (20;6);"Layout Coach Seating...............1"
  PRINT AT (20;8);"Seat Bookings.....................2"
  PRINT AT (20;10);"Show Totals......................3"
  PRINT AT (20;12);"Current Seating List.............4"
  PRINT AT (20;15);"Exit from Program................5"

  opt$=""
  WHILE opt$<"1" OR opt$>"5"
    opt$=INKEY$
  WEND

  opt=VAL(opt$)
  ON opt GOSUB layout,book,total,list,exit
UNTIL opt=5
END

LABEL layout
CLS
INPUT "Maximum number of rows ";rows
INPUT "Maximum number of seats across ";cross
CLS
  REM calculate grid size
gridx=INT(600/(rows+2))
IF gridx>50 THEN gridx=50
 REM minibuses cause display problems
endx=gridx*(rows+1)
gridy=gridx/2:endy=gridy*(cross+1)
seatx=gridx*.8:seaty=gridy*.8
xdiff=(gridx-seatx)/2:ydiff=(gridy-seaty)/2
```

```
 REM draw grid
FOR r=1 TO rows+1
  LINE gridx*r;gridy,gridx*r;endy
NEXT r
FOR c=1 TO cross+1
  LINE gridx;gridy*c,endx;gridy*c
NEXT c
 REM draw seats
FOR r=1 TO rows
  FOR c=1 TO cross
    BOX gridx*r+xdiff;gridy*c+ydiff,seatx,seaty COLOUR 2 FILL
    coach(r,c)=2
  NEXT c
NEXT r
PRINT AT (29;2);"Move with Mouse"
PRINT AT (25;4);"Click to remove/replace"
PRINT AT (20;6);"Click to code seats, or when done"
LINE 10;160,100;160,100;180,10;180,10;160 WIDTH 5
PRINT AT (3;4);"SEAT CODES"
LINE 540;160,630;160,630;180,540;180,540;160 WIDTH 5
PRINT AT (70;4);"FINISHED"

finished=0
REPEAT
  WHILE BUTTON(1)=-1:WEND
  xm=XMOUSE
  ym=YMOUSE*YPIXEL
  IF xm>gridx AND xm<endx AND ym>gridy AND ym<endy THEN GOSUB getseat
  IF xm>10 AND xm<100 AND ym>160 AND ym<180 THEN GOSUB seatcodes
  IF xm>540 AND xm<630 AND ym>160 AND ym<180 THEN finished=1
UNTIL finished

GOSUB getname
INPUT AT(4;21);"Description of this tour ";trip$
PRINT AT(4;21);STRING$(50," ");
INPUT AT(4;21);"Seat price ";price
fileflag=1
RETURN

LABEL getseat
r=INT(xm/gridx):c=INT(ym/gridy)
oldcol=coach(r,c)
newcol=0:IF oldcol=0 THEN newcol=2
BOX gridx*r+xdiff;gridy*c+ydiff,seatx,seaty COLOUR newcol FILL
coach(r,c)=newcol
RETURN
```

```
LABEL seatcodes
row$="A"
seatnumber=0
FOR r=1 TO rows
  cross$="1"
  FOR c=1 TO cross
    xrow=gridx*r+xdiff:ycol=gridy*c+ydiff
    IF coach(r,c)=0 THEN GOTO nextc
    seatnumber=seatnumber+1
    seat$(seatnumber,1)=row$+cross$
    seat$(seatnumber,2)=""
    MOVE xrow;ycol:PRINT seat$(seatnumber,1)
    cross$=CHR$(ASC(cross$)+1)
    seat(seatnumber,1)=r:seat(seatnumber,2)=c
    seat(seatnumber,3)=2
    LABEL nextc
  NEXT c
  row$=CHR$(ASC(row$)+1)
NEXT r
RETURN

LABEL book
CLS
IF file$<>"" THEN GOSUB oldtour ELSE GOSUB gettour
CLS
endx=0:endy=0
FOR s=1 TO seatnumber
  xrow=seat(s,1)*gridx:ycol=seat(s,2)*gridy
  IF xrow>endx THEN endx=xrow
  IF ycol>endy THEN endy=ycol
  BOX xrow;ycol,seatx,seaty COLOUR seat(s,3) FILL
  MOVE xrow;ycol:PRINT seat$(s,1);
NEXT s
endx=endx+seatx:endy=endy+seaty
PRINT AT (20;2);"Click to update seats, or when done"
LINE 540;160,630;160,630;180,540;180,540;160 WIDTH 5
PRINT AT (70;4);"FINISHED"
finished=0
REPEAT
  WHILE BUTTON(1)=-1:WEND
  xm=XMOUSE
  ym=YMOUSE*1.13
  IF xm>gridx AND xm<endx AND ym>gridy AND ym<endy THEN GOSUB updateseat
  IF xm>540 AND xm<630 AND ym>160 AND ym<180 THEN finished=1
UNTIL finished
fileflag=1
RETURN
```

```
LABEL oldtour
PRINT "Current Tour ";LEFT$(file$,8);". Use this?"
INPUT ans$
IF UPPER$(ans$)="N" THEN GOSUB gettour
RETURN

LABEL gettour
REPEAT
  GOSUB getname
  x$=FIND$(file$)
  IF x$=file$ THEN GOTO getout
  PRINT AT(1;7);"Tours on File"
  filenumber=1
  REPEAT
    x$=FIND$("*.BUS",filenumber)
    PRINT LEFT$(x$,8)
    filenumber=filenumber+1
  UNTIL x$=""
  IF filenumber=2 THEN PRINT "None present"
  LABEL getout
UNTIL x$=file$ OR filenumber=2
IF x$="" THEN RETURN
OPEN #5 INPUT file$
INPUT #5,trip$
INPUT #5,price
INPUT #5,seatx,seaty,gridx,gridy,seatnumber
FOR s=1 TO seatnumber
  INPUT #5,rec$
  seat$(s,1)=LEFT$(rec$,2)
  rec$=MID$(rec$,3,LEN(rec$))
  slash=INSTR(rec$,"/")
  seat$(s,2)=LEFT$(rec$,slash-1)
  rec$=MID$(rec$,slash+1,LEN(rec$))
  slash=INSTR(rec$,"/")
  seat(s,1)=VAL(LEFT$(rec$,slash-1))
  rec$=MID$(rec$,slash+2,LEN(rec$))
  seat(s,2)=VAL(LEFT$(rec$,LEN(rec$)-1))
  seat(s,3)=VAL(RIGHT$(rec$,1))
NEXT s
CLOSE #5
RETURN

LABEL getname
PRINT AT(4;21);"Tour filename:_____"
INPUT AT(18;21);file$
WHILE LEN(file$)<8:file$=file$+" ":WEND
```

```
IF LEN(file$)>8 THEN file$=LEFT$(file$,8)
file$=UPPER$(file$)+".BUS"
RETURN


LABEL updateseat
r=(xm\gridx):c=(ym\gridy)
this=0
FOR s=1 TO seatnumber
  IF seat(s,1)<>r THEN GOTO nextseat
  IF seat(s,2)<>c THEN GOTO nextseat
  this=s

  LABEL nextseat
NEXT s
IF this=0 THEN RETURN
xrow=r*gridx:ycol=c*gridy
xseat=xrow+seatx:yseat=ycol+seaty
LINE xrow;ycol,xrow;yseat,xseat;yseat,xseat;ycol,xrow;ycol
LINE 200;132,440;132,440;176,200;176,200;132 WIDTH 5
PRINT AT(28;4);"Empty.............1"
PRINT AT(28;5);"Reserve...........2"
PRINT AT(28;6);"Fully Paid........3"
REPEAT
  ky=-1
  WHILE ky=-1:ky=INKEY:WEND
UNTIL ky>48 AND ky<52
IF ky=49 THEN seat(this,3)=2:seat$(this,2)=""
IF ky=50 THEN GOSUB reserve
IF ky=51 THEN GOSUB pay
BOX xrow;ycol,seatx,seaty COLOUR seat(this,3) FILL
MOVE xrow;ycol:PRINT seat$(this,1)
BOX 196;128,248,52 COLOUR 0 FILL
RETURN


LABEL reserve
seat(this,3)=3
INPUT AT(28;7);"Name ";seat$(this,2)
RETURN


LABEL pay
seat(this,3)=4
FOR n=4 TO 6:PRINT AT(28;n);"                    ":NEXT n
PRINT AT(28;4);"Seat reserved for"
IF seat$(this,2)<>"" THEN GOSUB correctname
IF seat$(this,2)="" THEN INPUT AT(28;7);"Name ";seat$(this,2)
GOSUB checkprint
```

```
PRINT #0,trip$
PRINT #0,"Seat No:";seat$(this,1)
PRINT #0,"Issued to:";seat$(this,2)
PRINT #0
RETURN

LABEL correctname
PRINT AT(28;5),seat$(this,2)
INPUT AT(28;6);"Correct ?";ans$
IF UPPER$(ans$)="N" THEN seat$(this,2)=""
RETURN

LABEL total
CLS
IF file$<>"" THEN GOSUB oldtour ELSE GOSUB gettour
empty=0:reserved=0:paid=0
FOR s=1 TO seatnumber
  IF seat(s,3)=2 THEN empty=empty+1
  IF seat(s,3)=3 THEN reserved=reserved+1
  IF seat(s,3)=4 THEN paid=paid+1
NEXT s
PRINT
PRINT trip$
PRINT "Seat Price..............f";price
PRINT "Empty Seats.............";empty
PRINT "Reserved but not paid...";reserved
PRINT "Seats Paid for..........";paid
PRINT "Booking Revenue.........f";paid*price
PRINT "Total seats on coach....";seatnumber
GOSUB anykey
RETURN

LABEL list
REPEAT
  CLS
  IF file$<>"" THEN GOSUB oldtour ELSE GOSUB gettour
  INPUT "Print on screen or paper (S/P) ";where$
UNTIL UPPER$(where$)="S" OR UPPER$(where$)="P"
IF UPPER$(where$)="S" THEN where=1 ELSE where=0
IF where=0 THEN GOSUB checkprint
PRINT #where,LEFT$(file$,8)
PRINT #where,trip$
PRINT #where,"Seat price....f";price
PRINT #where,"Seat";TAB(10);"Reserved for";TAB(40);"Paid?"
FOR s=1 TO seatnumber
  name$=seat$(s,2):IF name$="" THEN name$="EMPTY"
```

117

```
  paid$=""
  IF seat(s,3)=3 THEN paid$="N" ELSE IF seat(s,3)=4 THEN paid$="Y"
  PRINT #where,seat$(s,1);TAB(10);name$;TAB(40);paid$
NEXT s
PRINT #where
IF where=1 THEN GOSUB anykey
RETURN


LABEL checkprint
FOR n=4 TO 7:PRINT AT(28;n);"                   ":NEXT n
PRINT AT(32;4);"Printer Ready?"
PRINT AT(28;5);"Press any key to print"
ky$=""
WHILE ky$="":ky$=INKEY$:WEND
RETURN


LABEL anykey
PRINT "Press Any Key to Continue"
ky$=""
WHILE ky$="":ky$=INKEY$:WEND
RETURN


LABEL exit
IF fileflag=0 THEN RETURN
OPEN #5 OUTPUT file$
PRINT #5,trip$
PRINT #5,price
PRINT #5,seatx,seaty,gridx,gridy,seatnumber
FOR s=1 TO seatnumber
  rec$=seat$(s,1)+seat$(s,2)
  rec$=rec$+"/"+STR$(seat(s,1))+"/"+STR$(seat(s,2))+STR$(seat(s,3))
  PRINT #5,rec$
NEXT s
CLOSE #5
RETURN
```

Chapter 10

Transformations

This is a mouse- and menu-driven program offering a range of two-dimensional transformations. Shapes are designed on-screen by pointing and clicking at the vertices. Lines drawn in error can be erased during the design stage; or for greater accuracy the co-ordinates of the vertices may be corrected later through an editing routine. Once defined, a shape may be enlarged, reflected in either or both axes, rotated or translated. Shapes may be filed on disk for future reference.

As well as demonstrating the principles of two-dimensional transformations, the program was also written as an exercise in window and mouse handling. All menus are presented in an overlaid window and selections are made by scrolling a highlight bar over the options and clicking on the required one. This part of the system works very well, but the comments made earlier (Chapter 8) about the redrawing of windows in Basic2 apply even more strongly here. Where you have a complex shape and have transformed it several times, data tends to be lost when the screen is restored after the upper window is closed. As the axes are always the first things to be drawn, these are also the first things to be abandoned in the redrawing — which can be irritating. This limitation means that you cannot use the program to produce intricate displays formed by multiple rotations and translations, though there is no problem with simpler screens.

Try the program as it stands, and if you find that the windows interfere with how you want to use it, then reserve a small area of the screen for your menus, and display them all there. This can be done in the same graphics window, or you can leave the small text window permanently open and simply CLS it at the end of each selection.

Program structure

Initialisation

    Initialise arrays for co-ordinates and options

Main loop

Main loop	*menus*
Trap mouse	
Open window to get option (Level 2)	*options*
Perform options (Level 1)	
Until exit flag set	

Options

Transform	*transform*
Enlarge, scale factors for x and y, redraw	*enlarge*
Reflect, in x, y or both, adjust and redraw	*reflect*
Rotate, angle in degrees	*rotate*
Single step, calculate and redraw	*onestep*
Multiple steps, loop of single steps	*multistep*
Translate, x and y translations, redraw	*translate*
Edit	*editing*
Create new, set up grid and screen prompts	*create*
Trap mouse	
On grid clicks define points	*plot__point*
Status line clicks erase/done	*erase__last*
Take backup of co-ordinate set	
Edit old	
Number points on shape	*editpara*
Display current co-ordinate values	
Get number to change and new values	
Clear screen	
Redraw grid and shape	*grid*
(Previous transformations erased)	
Restore	
Put co-ords back to original values	*restorepara*
File	*filing*
Save	
Open window to get filename	*savepara*
Save no. of points and their co-ords	
Load	
Open window to get filename	*loadpara*

Load number of points and co-ords
Make backup copy of co-ords

Exit
If exit confirmed, set flag

Subroutines

Grid   *grid*
Draw axes and mark divisions

Redraw   *redraw*
Transfer co-ordinates to temps
Check for edges and trim if necessary
Plot first point, draw lines between subsequent pairs

Window for Level 2 options   *window2*
Display menu
Trap mouse
Highlight option under pointer   *reverse__display*
Until clicked
Return option number

Notes

Transformations

Here we are using a Cartesian co-ordinate system, i.e. one that has negative as well as positive values for x and y. The origin of the axes (0,0) is at the centre of the screen. The graphics window is defined to match this system, with the co-ordinates scaled to pixel size:

```
USER SPACE 640,180
USER ORIGIN 320,90
```

As the 1512 pixels are twice as high as they are wide, a square 100 points wide would have to be 50 high to look right on screen. Most of the time this makes not the slightest bit of difference, as the numerical value of the co-ordinates can be happily ignored by the user. However, the Create and Edit routines do display the numbers on screen and as the discrepancy between the vertical and the y values could be misleading, all y values are doubled for display.

Users of the 1640 may prefer to define the SPACE as 320 high and set the ORIGIN at 320,160. The display doubling can then be cut out of the Create and Edit routines.

Enlargements can be tackled in two ways. The co-ordinates can either be scaled relative to the origin of the axes, or relative to the first vertex. The first method is the simplest; there each co-ordinate pair is multiplied by the x and y factors, respectively. The effect is not only to enlarge the shape, but also to move it further from the origin. Thus, a square with bottom left and top right corners at (20,20) and (50,50), enlarged by ×2 in both directions, would have those same corners at (40,40) and (100,100):

```
x(coord)=x(coord)*scalex
y(coord)=y(coord)*scaley
```

Where the transformation is relative to a vertex or to a point within the shape (and the first point is as good a one as any to use) , it will be enlarged just the same, but will not be moved across the grid. A square with corners at (20,20) and (50,50), would have the same corners at (20,20) and (80,80) after doubling. The lines are:

```
x(coord)=x(1)+(x(coord)-x(1))*scalex)
y(coord)=y(1)+(y(coord)-y(1))*scaley)
```

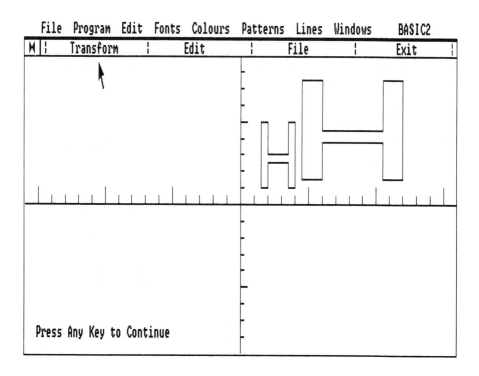

For example:

Co-ordinate	Original	Calculation	Enlarged
x(1)	20	20+(20-20)*2	20
x(3)	50	20+(50-20)*2	80

Reflections can be made with the 'mirror lines' on the x-axis, or the y-axis. The 'both' option is a compound of the two. You may wish to add routines to perform the two other common reflections, in the lines 'x = y' (that is, the diagonal sloping up and right through the origin) and 'x = −y' (the downward sloping diagonal). They are simple enough to manage. To reflect the shape in x = y, set up a loop to work through all the co-ordinates and swap the x and y values:

```
SWAP x(coord),y(coord)
```

To reflect in x = −y, the co-ordinates need to be swapped and then made negative. Hence, within the loop you would need:

```
SWAP x(coord),y(coord)
x(coord)=x(coord)*-1
y(coord)=y(coord)*-1
```

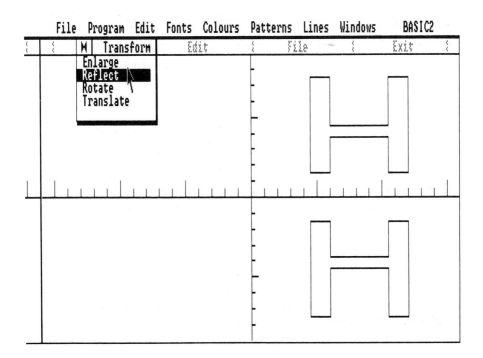

123

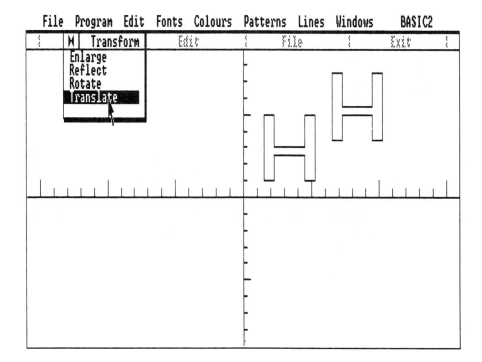

Translations require only that the x and y movements should be added onto the existing values.

Rotations are perhaps the most complicated transformations to manage. The rotations can be about the origin of the axes, as they are here, or centred on a point within the shape. We will return to this approach later.

The basic formulae to rotate a point through an angle are:

```
x(new)=x*COS(angle)+y*SIN(angle)
y(new)=y*COS(angle)-x*SIN(angle)
```

The actual formulae are slightly different for several reasons. First, the original x and y values are needed in both calculations; therefore the first result must be stored in a temporary variable. Secondly, the relative difference in the scale of the axes (50 points high is equivalent to 100 wide), means that the shape would be distorted by the rotation. To overcome this, the y values are doubled in the expressions, then halved afterwards. (Users of the 1640 who have opted for the 640 × 350 USER SPACE can ignore this.) Lastly, the same calculation routines are used for single or multiple rotations, and to save the computer from having to work out the sines and cosines every time, they are calculated once at the start and stored in variables. The resulting lines are therefore:

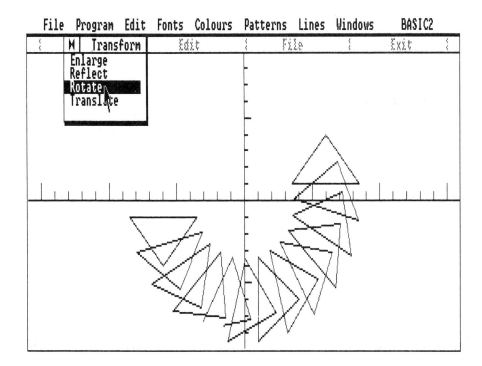

```
tempy=y(coord)*2*cosangle  - x(coord)*sinangle
x(coord)=x(coord)*cosangle + y(coord)*2*sinangle
y(coord)=tempy/2
```

You can use the present program to rotate a shape about a point within itself by moving the shape until it is centred on the origin. The normal rotation routine will then work perfectly well for this purpose. If you want to be able to rotate a shape about itself, wherever it is on screen, then a new routine is needed.

This should start by collecting the co-ordinates of the centre of rotation — perhaps by mouse click. These could be stored in *midx* and *midy*. Then, before a point is transformed, adjust its co-ordinates so that they are relative to this point rather than to the origin. Finally, the new values must be readjusted so that they are once more relative to the origin. The routine becomes:

```
x=x(coord)-midx
y=y(coord)-midy
tempy=y*2*cosangle-x*sinangle
x=x*cosangle+y*2*sinangle
y=tempy/2
x(coord)=x+midx
y(coord)=y+midy
```

Transformation program

```
REM transformations

LABEL initialise
DRIVE "B":REM ignore on one drive systems
OPTION DEGREES
DIM x(100),y(100),a(100),b(100)
DIM opts(3),title$(3),opt$(3,8)

FOR loop=0 TO 3
  READ opts(loop),title$(loop)
  FOR choice=1 TO opts(loop)
    READ opt$(loop,choice)
  NEXT choice
NEXT loop

REM menu 1
DATA 4,Transform," Enlarge "," Reflect "," Rotate   "," Translate "
REM menu 2
DATA 4,Edit," Create New  "," Edit Old    "," Clear Screen"," Restore      "
REM menu 3
DATA 2,File, " Save         "," Load         "
REM menu 4
DATA 2,Exit, " Yes          "," No           "

SCREEN #1 GRAPHICS 640 FIXED, 200 FIXED
WINDOW #1 FULL ON
USER SPACE 640,180
USER ORIGIN 320;90
WINDOW #1 OPEN

exit=0
GOSUB grid
WHILE exit=0
  choice2=0
  WINDOW  TITLE  "¦    Transform    ¦      Edit      ¦       File
  - ¦       Exit      ¦"
  y=0
  WHILE y<80
    x=XMOUSE-320:y=YMOUSE-90:status=BUTTON(1)
  WEND
  GOSUB menus
  IF choice2>0 THEN GOSUB options
WEND
END
```

```
LABEL menus
choice=INT((x+288)/144)
IF choice>3 THEN RETURN
xedge=choice*144+56
height=opts(choice)
title$=title$(choice)
num_opts=opts(choice)
FOR loop=1 TO num_opts
  option$(loop)=opt$(choice,loop)
NEXT loop
wide=144
GOSUB window2
RETURN

LABEL options
ON choice+1 GOSUB transform,editing,filing,exit
RETURN

LABEL transform
ON choice2 GOSUB enlarge,reflect,rotate,translate
RETURN

LABEL enlarge
INPUT AT (2;21);"Scale Factor for x ";scalex
PRINT AT (2;21);"                              "
INPUT AT (2;21);"Scale Factor for y ";scaley
FOR coord=1 TO count
  REM scaling relative to origin
  x(coord)=x(coord)*scalex
  y(coord)=y(coord)*scaley
  REM Alternative for scaling relative to first point
  REM x(coord)=x(1)+((x(coord)-x(1))*scalex)
  REM y(coord)=y(1)+((y(coord)-y(1))*scaley)
NEXT coord
GRAPHICS COLOUR 2
GOSUB redraw
GRAPHICS COLOUR 1
GOSUB anykey
RETURN

LABEL reflect
PRINT AT (2;21);" Reflect in x, y or (b)oth"
REPEAT
  a$=UPPER$(INKEY$)
UNTIL a$="X" OR a$="Y" OR a$="B"
```

```
FOR coord=1 TO count
  IF a$="X" OR a$="B" THEN y(coord)=y(coord)*-1
  IF a$="Y" OR a$="B" THEN x(coord)=x(coord)*-1
NEXT coord
GRAPHICS COLOUR 3
GOSUB redraw
GRAPHICS COLOUR 1
GOSUB anykey
RETURN


LABEL rotate
INPUT AT (2;21);"Angle of Rotation ";anglerot
PRINT AT (2;21);"(S)ingle or (M)ultiple steps"
REPEAT
  a$=UPPER$(INKEY$)
UNTIL a$="S" OR a$="M"
PRINT AT (2;21);"                            "
IF a$="S" THEN GOSUB onestep ELSE GOSUB multistep
GOSUB anykey
RETURN


LABEL onestep
cosangle=COS(anglerot):sinangle=SIN(anglerot)
GRAPHICS COLOUR 4
GOSUB calc_rotate
GRAPHICS COLOUR 1
RETURN


LABEL multistep
INPUT AT (2;21);"Number of steps ";numsteps
anglerot=anglerot/numsteps
cosangle=COS(anglerot):sinangle=SIN(anglerot)
GRAPHICS COLOUR 4
FOR rotor=1 TO numsteps
  GOSUB calc_rotate
NEXT rotor
GRAPHICS COLOUR 1
RETURN


LABEL calc_rotate
FOR coord=1 TO count
  tempy=y(coord)*2*cosangle-x(coord)*sinangle
  x(coord)=x(coord)*cosangle+y(coord)*2*sinangle
  y(coord)=tempy/2
NEXT coord
GOSUB redraw
RETURN
```

```
LABEL translate
INPUT AT (2;21);"x translation ";xtran
PRINT AT (2;21);"                    "
INPUT AT (2;21);"y translation ";ytran
PRINT AT (2;21);"                    "
FOR coord=1 TO count
  x(coord)=x(coord)+xtran
  y(coord)=y(coord)+ytran
NEXT coord
GRAPHICS COLOUR 5
GOSUB redraw
GRAPHICS COLOUR 1
GOSUB anykey
RETURN


LABEL editing
ON choice2 GOSUB create,editpara,grid,restorepara
RETURN


LABEL create
count=1
GOSUB grid
WINDOW TITLE "[Erase]    Press Button to Plot Point            [Done]    "
LINE -300;-84,-72;-84,-72;-72,-300;-72,-300;-84
done=0
x=XMOUSE-320:y=YMOUSE-90:x1=x:y1=y


REPEAT
  x=XMOUSE-320:y=YMOUSE-90:status=BUTTON(1)
  IF y>80 AND x>-212 AND x<-160 AND status=0 THEN GOSUB erase_last
  IF y>80 AND x>180 AND x<220 AND status=0 THEN done=1
  IF y<80 AND status=0 THEN GOSUB plot_point
  IF x1<>x OR y1<>y THEN PRINT AT(4;21);"x ";x;" ":PRINT  AT(14;21);"y ";
  -   y*2;" ":x1=x:y1=y
UNTIL done
count=count-1
FOR coord=1 TO count
  a(coord)=x(coord)
  b(coord)=y(coord)
NEXT coord
GOSUB grid
RETURN


LABEL plot_point
PRINT AT(24;21);"No";count;" "
IF count=1 THEN PLOT x;y ELSE LINE x(count-1);y(count-1),x;y
```

```
x(count)=x:y(count)=y:count=count+1
WHILE BUTTON(1)=0:WEND
RETURN


LABEL erase_last
IF count=1 THEN RETURN
count=count-1:PRINT AT(24;21);"No";count;" "
IF count=1 THEN PLOT x(count);y(count) MODE 3 ELSE
-    LINE x(count);y(count),x(count-1);y(count-1) MODE 3
WHILE BUTTON(1)=0:WEND
RETURN


LABEL editpara
FOR coord=1 TO count
  x1=x(coord):IF x1>310 THEN x1=310
  IF x1<-310 THEN x1=-310
  y1=y(coord):IF y1>85 THEN y1=85
  IF y1<-85 THEN y1=-85
  MOVE x1;y1:PRINT coord POINTS (8)
  IF count<18 THEN col=1 ELSE col=20
  PRINT AT(col;coord);coord;" x ";INT(x(coord));" y ";INT(y(coord)*2)
NEXT coord
INPUT AT(2;18);"Number to change";num
WHILE num>0
  INPUT AT(2;19);"New x value ";x(num)
  INPUT AT(2;20);"New y value ";n:y(num)=n/2
  PRINT AT(2;18);STRING$(25," ")
  PRINT AT(2;19);STRING$(25," ")
  PRINT AT (2;20);"Type 0 to exit     "
  INPUT AT(2;18);"Number to change";num
WEND
GOSUB grid
RETURN


LABEL restorepara
FOR coord=1 TO count
  x(coord)=a(coord)
  y(coord)=b(coord)
NEXT coord
GOSUB grid
RETURN


LABEL filing
ON choice2 GOSUB savepara,loadpara
RETURN
```

```
LABEL savepara
WINDOW #2 CLOSE
SCREEN #2 TEXT 24 FIXED, 4 FIXED INFORMATION OFF
WINDOW #2 PLACE 240,90
WINDOW #2 OPEN
PRINT #2,AT (1;2);"FILENAME FOR SAVING"
PRINT #2,AT (1;3);"Name:_____"
INPUT #2,AT (5;3);file$
IF LEN(file$)>8 THEN file$=LEFT$(file$,8)
WHILE LEN(file$)<8:file$=file$+" ":WEND
file$=UPPER$(file$)+".XY_"
WINDOW #2 CLOSE
OPEN #5 OUTPUT file$
PRINT #5,count
FOR coord=1 TO count
  PRINT #5,x(coord),y(coord)
NEXT coord
CLOSE #5
RETURN


LABEL loadpara
WINDOW #2 CLOSE
SCREEN #2 TEXT 24 FIXED, 4 FIXED INFORMATION OFF
WINDOW #2 PLACE 240,90
WINDOW #2 OPEN
found=0
REPEAT
  PRINT #2,AT(1;2);"FILENAME FOR LOADING"
  PRINT #2,AT (1;3);"Name:_____"
  INPUT #2,AT(5;3);file$
  IF LEN(file$)>8 THEN file$=LEFT$(file$,8)
  WHILE LEN(file$)<8:file$=file$+" ":WEND
  file$=UPPER$(file$)+".XY_"
  x$=FIND$(file$):IF x$=file$ THEN found=1
UNTIL found
WINDOW #2 CLOSE
OPEN #5 INPUT file$
INPUT #5,count
FOR coord=1 TO count
  INPUT #5,x(coord),y(coord)
  a(coord)=x(coord)
  b(coord)=y(coord)
NEXT coord
CLOSE #5
GOSUB grid
RETURN
```

```
LABEL exit
IF choice2=1 THEN exit=1 ELSE exit=0
RETURN

LABEL grid
CLS
LINE -319;0,319;0
LINE 0;-89,0;89
FOR x=-300 TO 300 STEP 20
  LINE x;0,x;5:IF INT(x/100)=x/100 THEN LINE x;5,x;10
NEXT x
FOR y=-80 TO 80 STEP 10
  LINE 0;y,5;y:IF INT(y/50)=y/50 THEN LINE 5;y,10;y
NEXT y

LABEL redraw

IF count=1 THEN RETURN

FOR coord=1 TO count
  x1=x(coord)
  IF x1>310 THEN x1=310
  IF x1<-310 THEN x1=-310
  y1=y(coord)
  IF y1>85 THEN y1=85
  IF y1<-85 THEN y1=-85
  IF coord=1 THEN PLOT x1;y1 ELSE LINE x2;y2,x1;y1
  x2=x1:y2=y1
NEXT coord
RETURN

LABEL window2
WINDOW #2 CLOSE
SCREEN #2 TEXT 15 FIXED, height FIXED INFORMATION OFF
WINDOW #2 PLACE xedge,180
WINDOW #2 TITLE title$
WINDOW #2 OPEN
FOR num=1 TO num_opts
  PRINT #2,option$(num)
NEXT num

temp=0:temp2=0:choice2=0:flag=-1:inbox=0

WHILE flag=-1
  flag=BUTTON(1)
  x=XMOUSE:y=YMOUSE
```

```
  IF x=>xedge AND x=<xedge+wide AND y<180 AND y>180-num_opts*8 THEN
  -   GOSUB reverse_display ELSE inbox=0
  IF flag=0 AND inbox<>0 THEN choice2=temp
WEND
WINDOW #2 CLOSE
RETURN


LABEL reverse_display
inbox=1
temp=INT((180-y)/8)+1:IF temp<1 THEN temp=1
IF temp=temp2 THEN RETURN
IF temp2<>0 THEN PRINT #2 AT(1;temp2);option$(temp2)
PRINT #2, AT(1;temp);EFFECTS (&X1000000);option$(temp)
temp2=temp
RETURN


LABEL anykey
PRINT AT(2;21);" Press Any Key to Continue         "
REPEAT
  a$=INKEY$
UNTIL a$<>""
PRINT AT(2;21);"                              "
RETURN
```

Chapter 11

Three-Dimension
Room Planner

Thinking about redecorating a room, buying new furniture or just rearranging what's already there? Why not see what it will look like before you start? Check that the wardrobe will fit before you strain your back shunting it from place to place. The room planner is here to save you time and trouble.

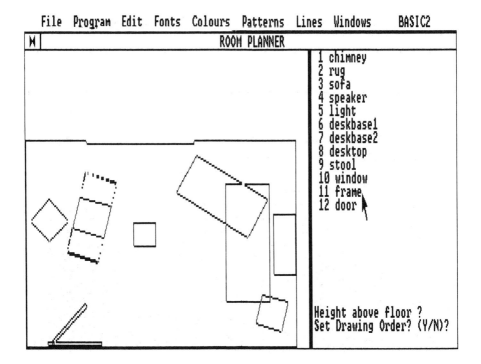

So much for the sales pitch. Now what exactly does this program do? It lets you define a room and the objects that will go in it − their sizes, colours and patterns. The room can have different colours and patterns on the floor, walls and ceiling; and while the basic shape must be rectangular, an L-shaped or other irregular room could be simulated by defining the intruding walls as 'objects'. Doors, windows, picture rails, chimney breasts and other fixtures can also be brought in as 'objects'. An object must be cuboid, but complex shapes such as tables and chairs can be created from sets of subordinate objects.

A two-dimensional floor plan routine allows each object to be positioned in the room, then rotated and slid around until it is in exactly the right place. Finally, the room can be viewed in three dimensions and turned so that you can view it from different sides. The room can be redefined at any time without losing the object set, and individual objects can be relocated, redefined or removed from the list. New objects can be also be added at a later date, and the whole design can be saved to disk for future reference or reworking.

It is a system that could well be used by a professional kitchen planning service or other fitted furniture retailer − some upgrading would be necessary as there are still a few raw edges that are less than user-friendly. More comprehensive error-trapping is needed and there are several areas where additional programming would make life easier for the non-specialist user. These things have not been included because the

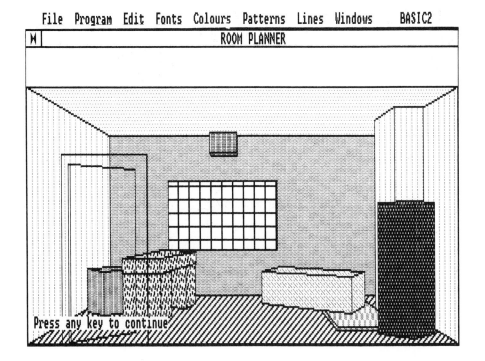

program is sufficiently complicated enough already. Three-dimensional representation inevitably involves some fairly complex algorithms, and all the more so where you have a set of individual objects that must be handled flexibly.

Program structure

Initialisation

    Initialise arrays and graphics screen

Main loop

    Display menu
    Perform options
    Until exit selected

Options

Define room	*room*
Get dimensions	
Calculate scale & co-ords of vertices	*setroom*
For floor, walls, ceiling	
Get colour & pattern	
Define objects	*objects*
Repeat	
Get object name	
If already defined, use old array number	
Else use next	
Get length	
If 0, then delete object from list	*deleteobject*
Get width, height, colour and pattern	
Scale dimensions and store	
Set flags to show not rotated, not sited on plan	
Until no more objects	

Fix layout   *plan*
   Draw floor plan outline
   Display object name and numbers
   Repeat
      Get object number
      If sited, draw in, else trap mouse to locate
      Wait for mouse or keypress — mouse to relocate
         'R' rotate object 15 degrees   *rotate*
         'E' fix location, get height off floor
      Calculate co-ordinates of vertices
   Until no more objects
   Offer jump direct to Set Draw Order

Set Draw Order   *draworder*
   Display object names and numbers
   Repeat
      Get object number
      Add to draw order list
      Mark off on screen
   Until all objects done

View room   *view*
   Scale floor, (3) walls and ceiling
   Send each in turn to be drawn   *drawshape*
   Take objects in drawing order
      Work out which faces should be drawn   *faces*
      Scale faces and send for drawing   *drawshape*

Change viewpoint   *change*
   Swap room length and width
   Move all walls round one
   For all objects
      Swap length and width
      Move all vertices co-ordinates round one corner

Save plan   *savefile*
   Get filename
   Save room dimensions, colours and patterns
   For every object
      Save name, corner co-ordinates
      Save colour, pattern and sizes

Load plan   *loadfile*
   Get filename
   Load file as saved
   Calculate room co-ordinates from dimensions

Notes

Three-dimensional representation

The representation of three-dimensional space in a computer system poses a number of interesting problems. Their solutions are usually a combination of theory and trial and error. Representation within memory is no problem — arrays of three dimensions can easily map the co-ordinates of objects in three-dimensional space. The difficulties arise when you try to display those objects on a two-dimensional screen.

The co-ordinate system used here has three axes, x, y and z, whose origin is at the centre-front of the room. The scale will depend upon the size of the room, and is designed so that whichever dimension is greatest (length, width or height) will have an internal size of 100 co-ordinate points:

```
LABEL setroom
   biggest=roomlength
   IF roomwidth>biggest THEN biggest=roomwidth
   IF roomheight>biggest THEN biggest=roomheight
scale=biggest/100
```

The x-axis runs across the width of the screen, the y-axis into the 'depth' of it, and the z-axis is vertical. This arrangement means that when a two-dimensional floor plan is required, only the more familiar x and y co-ordinates are used. Because of the way that perspective is handled, the origin of the x and z axes is equivalent to the observer's eye position within the room. For simplicity this has been set at the mid-points of the length and height, but a more realistic representation could be obtained if the origin was set in the middle of a doorway or window within the 'front' wall, approximately 1.5 metres high in real terms.

```
x=roomlength/scale
midx=x/2
y=roomwidth/scale
z=roomheight/scale
midz=z/2
```

To obtain a sense of perspective, the x and z co-ordinates of distant objects are scaled down to bring them closer to the origin. The degree of scaling is exponentially related to the distance of the object from the front of the screen. The formulae used are of the type:

```
screen_x=x*perspective_factor^y/100
```

Experimentation has shown that a perspective factor of 0.5 looks right. (This is written into the variable *per* at the beginning of the program. You may wish to adjust this to test the effects of different values.) Where the factor is 0.5, it would mean that an object at the maximum distance — the back of a square room — would be displayed at half its proper size.

The shape of the room, and the position and size of all objects within it are stored by calculating the co-ordinates of corners. These are always numbered in the same way, with '1' at the bottom front left corner, continuing clockwise round to 4 at the bottom front right, then 5 to 8 holding the equivalent top corners.

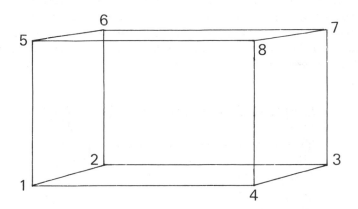

The room's co-ordinates in display terms can now be calculated:

```
pers=per^(y/100)
rmx(1)=-midx:rmy(1)=0:rmz(1)=-midz
rmx(2)=-midx*pers:rmy(2)=y:rmz(2)=-midz*pers
rmx(3)=midx*pers:rmy(3)=y:rmz(3)=-midz*pers
rmx(4)=midx:rmy(4)=0:rmz(4)=-midz
rmx(5)=-midx:rmy(5)=0:rmz(5)=midz
....
```

Some further scaling will be needed later to adjust these co-ordinates for display on screen, but the proportions and relative positions are fixed. The USER SPACE has been set to 640 by 200. During the floor plan routine, *plan*, one side of the screen is reserved for data entry and messages, leaving an effective screen area of approximately 400 across by 200 high. On transfer to the screen, the room's x,y co-ordinates will be translated to bring the origin down to the bottom left, then multiplied by 4 and 2, respectively. Given that the pixels are twice as high as they are wide, the final co-ordinates will be in the right place for a properly scaled display. When the room is viewed in three dimensions and the full width of the screen is used, the final scaling will be 6.4 in the horizontal plane and 3.2 in the vertical.

In *view*, the room appears on screen as a set of five shapes — floor, ceiling and three walls. Each of these shapes is defined by the co-ordinates of its four corners, with those of the walls held in the array *roomside(4,4)*. The corner numbers are READ into this array at the start of the program — for example, *roomside(1,1 to 4)* is the series 1,2,6,5, which gives the vertices of the left wall. For drawing, the co-ordinates of each surface's corners are passed to the arrays *x* and *z*; the colour to *col* and the pattern number to *pat*. The *drawshape* subroutine then draws and outlines the surface:

```
SHAPE x(1);z(1),x(2);z(2),x(3);z(3),x(4);z(4),x(1);z(1)
   COLOUR col FILL WITH pat
LINE x(1);z(1),x(2);z(2),x(3);z(3),x(4);z(4),x(1);z(1) COLOUR 1
```

A rather more complex sequence of calculations is needed to fix the objects' positions in three-dimensional space then display them on screen. First, the object's dimensions are collected and stored in the array *obsize(50,4)*, where the first subscript is the object number and the rest are length, width, height (all scaled to the room's co-ordinate system) and degree of rotation.

When the object is sited in the *plan* routine, its front left corner is at the position given by the mouse's x,y values and the other three corners of its base are calculated from its length and width. (Note that *oblength* and *obwidth* are multiplied up by 4 and 2 as the co-ordinates are needed for screen display at this stage.)

```
oblength=obsize(num,1)*4:obwidth=obsize(num,2)*2
x(1)=x:y(1)=y
x(2)=x:y(2)=y+obwidth
x(3)=x+oblength:y(3)=y+obwidth
x(4)=x+oblength:y(4)=y
```

Once sited on the plan, the object may be slid to new positions or rotated. The calculations used here are almost identical to those in the Transformations program, but note that rotations are managed in 15-degree clockwise increments. The number of fractional turns are recorded and should the object be rotated through a full quarter turn the co-ordinates of all corners are exchanged. This ensures that corner 1 is always at the front left or on the left-hand side. This is important at the display stage.

On exit from the siting routine, the planner will be asked for the object's height above the floor (stored in *upheight*). From this, and from the x,y values of the floor plan, the co-ordinates of all eight corners in three-dimensional space can be calculated and stored in the arrays *obx()*, *oby()* and *obz()*. (Note that the x,y co-ordinates are scaled down from their screen values and that the origin is moved to the centre of three-dimensional space.)

```
upheight=(upheight/scale)
FOR n=1 TO 4
    obx(num,n)=x(n)/4-midx
    oby(num,n)=y(n)/2
    obz(num,n)=upheight-midz
    obx(num,n+4)=x(n)/4-midx
    oby(num,n+4)=y(n)/2
    obz(num,n+4)=upheight+obsize(num,3)-midz
NEXT n
```

In the *view* routine, it is only necessary to draw those surfaces of the object that are visible, not all six. In fact, it is important that the 'hidden' surfaces are not drawn as they would confuse the image. Which ones are visible depends upon the object's position in relation to the origin (the viewpoint), and whether or not the object has been rotated. Thus, if an object is flat on to the front of the screen and in the lower right quadrant, its front, left and top surfaces can be seen; while one sitting at an angle in the upper centre of the screen would have its front, right and lower surfaces visible.

The surfaces have been numbered as shown:

1 = Front
2 = Left
3 = Right
4 = Bottom
5 = Top

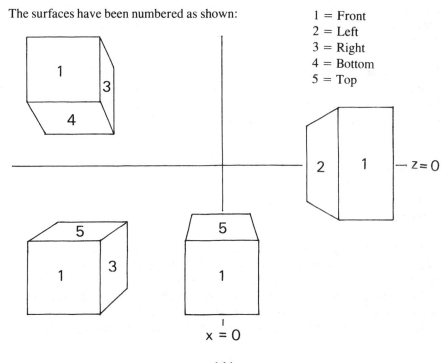

141

The back surface will never be visible. The *objects* section of the *view* routine checks the position and orientation of the current (*n*) object and transfers to *face()* the numbers of the three surfaces to be drawn:

```
face(1)=1
face(2)=0
IF oby(n,2)>oby(n,3)+0.1 THEN face(2)=3
- ELSE IF obx(n,3)<0 THEN face(2)=3
- ELSE IF obx(n,1)>0 THEN face(2)=2
face(3)=0
IF obz(n,5)<0 THEN face(3)=5
- ELSE IF obz(n,1)>0 THEN face(3)=4
```

face(1) is always 1 as the front will always be drawn. *face(2)* will be the right side (3) either if the object is at an angle, or if its right side is to the left of the centre line. The latter is tested by the x co-ordinate of corner 3 − IF obx(n,3)<0. The left side will be shown if the whole object is to the right of the centre. Where the object straddles the centre, neither side will be shown.

In the same way, the top surface will be visible if the whole object is below the horizontal axis; the bottom if the object is above it and neither if it is in the middle.

The *faces* routine finds the numbers of the corners of each surface, by reading through the *facedata* until the relevant part is reached. So, where the left-hand side (surface 2) is to be drawn, the values 1, 5, 8 and 4 would be read into the *dummy*, clearing the way for 1, 2, 6 and 5 − to be used for the *corners* of the left side:

```
LABEL facedata
    DATA 1,5,8,4,1,2,6,5,3,4,8,7,1,2,3,4,5,6,7,8

LABEL faces
    FOR num=1 TO 3
        readit=0
        WHILE readit<(face(num)-1)*4
            READ dummy
            readit=readit+1
        WEND
```

To find the x and z co-ordinates for the screen display, the perspective factor is calculated from the y value of each corner, then applied to the x and z values. They are then transposed to bring the origin down to the bottom left, and finally scaled up to screen size:

```
FOR c=1 TO 4
    READ corner
    pers=per^(oby(n,corner)/100)
    x(c)=(obx(n,corner)*pers+midx)*6.4
    z(c)=(obz(n,corner)*pers+midz)*3.2
NEXT c
```

Setting the drawing order

As it stands, the program requires the user to set the order in which the objects are to be drawn, and, clearly, the most satisfactory order is going to be furthermost first. Which objects are at the back does, of course, change as the viewpoint is altered, so it is necessary to reset the drawing order every time the room is rotated. This is a bit of a nuisance, and the process could do with automation. It has not been done here because it involves some fairly heavy programming and it was felt that the program already has more than enough complexities.

To set the draw order properly you need to check the position of objects along both the y and the x axes. While the main priority must be that those nearest the back are drawn first, it is also the case that those nearer to the centre of the screen, i.e. to the viewpoint, should be drawn after those closer to the sides. The way that an object is rotated may also affect the visibility of other objects behind and to the side of it.

Room planner program

```
DRIVE "B"

DIM roomside(4,4):REM room side coordinates
DIM ob$(50),obx(50,8),oby(50,8),obz(50,8),obcol(50),obpat(50),obsize(50,4)
 REM up to 50 objects - name,coordinates,colour,pattern and size
DIM order(50):REM drawing order
count=0:REM object count
per=0.5:REM perspective factor
FOR side=1 TO 4
  FOR corner=1 TO 4
    READ roomside(side,corner)
  NEXT corner
NEXT side
DATA 1,2,6,5,2,3,7,6,3,4,8,7,4,1,5,8
OPTION DEGREES

LABEL begin

SCREEN #1 GRAPHICS 640 FIXED,200 FIXED
USER SPACE 640,200
exit=0
WINDOW #1 FULL ON
WINDOW #1 OPEN
WINDOW TITLE "ROOM PLANNER"

WHILE exit=0
  CLS
  PRINT AT (25;2);"DEFINE ROOM.............1"
  PRINT AT (25;4);"DEFINE OBJECTS..........2"
  PRINT AT (25;6);"FIX LAYOUT..............3"
  PRINT AT (25;8);"SET DRAWING ORDER.......4"
  PRINT AT (25;10);"VIEW ROOM...............5"
  PRINT AT (25;12);"CHANGE VIEWPOINT........6"
  PRINT AT (25;14);"SAVE PLAN...............7"
  PRINT AT (25;16);"LOAD PLAN...............8"
  PRINT AT (25;18);"EXIT FROM PROGRAM.......9"
```

```
   REPEAT
     opt$=INKEY$
   UNTIL opt$>="1" AND opt$<="9"
   opt=VAL(opt$)
   IF opt<6 THEN CLS
   ON opt GOSUB room,objects,plan,draworder,view,change,saver,loader,exit
WEND
END


LABEL room
PRINT "Maximum Room Dimensions (in Centimetres)"
INPUT "Length ";roomlength
INPUT "Width ";roomwidth
INPUT "Height ";roomheight
IF roomlength*roomwidth*roomheight=0 THEN GOTO room:REM crude check
GOSUB setroom
PRINT "Colour Scheme"
INPUT "Floor Colour Number ";floorcol
INPUT "Floor Pattern Number ";floorpat
FOR side=1 TO 4
  PRINT "Colour for wall ";side;" ";
  INPUT wallcol(side)
  PRINT "Pattern for wall ";side;" ";
  INPUT wallpat(side)
NEXT side
INPUT "Ceiling Colour Number ";ceilingcol
INPUT "Ceiling Pattern Number ";ceilingpat
GOSUB anykey
RETURN


LABEL setroom
biggest=roomlength
IF roomwidth>biggest THEN biggest=roomwidth
IF roomheight>biggest THEN biggest=roomheight
scale = biggest/100
x=roomlength/scale
midx=x/2
y=roomwidth/scale
z=roomheight/scale
midz=z/2
```

```
 REM perspective depends on roomwidth
pers=per^(y/100)
 REM co-ordinates of corners in 3-D space
rmx(1)=-midx:rmy(1)=0:rmz(1)=-midz
rmx(2)=-midx*pers:rmy(2)=y:rmz(2)=-midz*pers
rmx(3)=midx*pers:rmy(3)=y:rmz(3)=-midz*pers
rmx(4)=midx:rmy(4)=0:rmz(4)=-midz
rmx(5)=-midx:rmy(5)=0:rmz(5)=midz
rmx(6)=-midx*pers:rmy(6)=y:rmz(6)=midz*pers
rmx(7)=midx*pers:rmy(7)=y:rmz(7)=midz*pers
rmx(8)=midx:rmy(8)=0:rmz(8)=midz
RETURN


LABEL objects
REPEAT
  num=0:count=count+1
  INPUT "Object name ";ob$(count)
  FOR loop=1 TO count-1
    IF ob$(count)=ob$(loop) THEN num=loop:PRINT "Redefining ";ob$(loop)
  NEXT loop
  IF num>0 THEN count=count-1 ELSE num=count
  IF count>50 THEN RETURN
  oblength=0
    PRINT "Length in Centimetres"
    INPUT "Length (0 to delete object)";oblength
    IF oblength=0 THEN GOSUB deleteobject:GOTO nextobject
    INPUT "Width ";obwidth
    INPUT "Height ";obheight
  obsize(num,1)=(oblength/scale)
  obsize(num,2)=(obwidth/scale)
  obsize(num,3)=(obheight/scale)
  obsize(num,4)=0:REM rotation counter
  obx(num,1)=0:REM not sited flag

  INPUT "Colour number ";obcol(num)
  INPUT "Pattern Number ";obpat(num)

  LABEL nextobject
  INPUT "Another? (Y/N) ";again$
  again$=UPPER$(again$)
UNTIL again$="N"
RETURN
```

```
LABEL deleteobject
count=count-1
FOR loop=num TO count
  ob$(loop)=ob$(loop+1)
  FOR n=1 TO 8
    obx(loop,n)=obx(loop+1,n)
    oby(loop,n)=oby(loop+1,n)
    obz(loop,n)=obz(loop+1,n)
  NEXT n
  obcol(loop)=obcol(loop+1):obpat(loop)=obpat(loop+1)
  FOR n=1 TO 4
    obsize(loop,n)=obsize(loop+1,n)
  NEXT n
NEXT loop
RETURN

LABEL plan
wide=roomwidth/scale*2
long=roomlength/scale*4
BOX 0;0,long,wide COLOUR 1
LINE 420;0,420;200 COLOUR 1 WIDTH 5
 REM display object names and numbers
num=18:IF count<18 THEN num=count
FOR loop=1 TO num
  PRINT AT (54;loop);loop;ob$(loop)
  IF loop+18<=count THEN PRINT AT (66;loop);loop+18;ob$(loop+18)
NEXT loop

REPEAT
  INPUT AT (54;20);" Object number ";num
  IF obx(num,1)<>0 THEN GOSUB sited ELSE GOSUB newsite
  rotated=obsize(num,4)
  PRINT AT (54;21);"R - Rotate, E - End"
  GRAPHICS MODE 3
  GRAPHICS CURSOR 1

  REPEAT
    GOSUB drawit
    ky$="":status=-1
    WHILE ky$="" AND status=-1
      x=XMOUSE:y=YMOUSE*YPIXEL
      status=BUTTON(1)
      IF status=0 THEN GOSUB moveit
      ky$=UPPER$(INKEY$)
```

```
      IF ky$="R" THEN GOSUB rotate
    WEND
  UNTIL ky$="E"

  GRAPHICS MODE 1
  PRINT AT (54;20);STRING$(24," ")
  PRINT AT (54;21);STRING$(24," ")
  INPUT AT (54;20);"Height above floor ";upheight
  upheight=(upheight/scale)
  FOR n=1 TO 4
    obx(num,n)=x(n)/4-midx
    oby(num,n)=y(n)/2
    obz(num,n)=upheight-midz
    obx(num,n+4)=x(n)/4-midx
    oby(num,n+4)=y(n)/2
    obz(num,n+4)=upheight+obsize(num,3)-midz
  NEXT n
  obsize(num,4)=rotated
  INPUT AT (54;21);"Another Object? (Y/N)";again$
  PRINT AT (54;20);STRING$(24," ")
  PRINT AT (54;21);STRING$(24," ")
  again$=UPPER$(again$)
UNTIL again$="N"
INPUT AT (54;21);"Set Drawing Order? (Y/N)";set$
set$=UPPER$(set$)
IF set$="N" THEN RETURN


LABEL draworder
LINE 420;0,420;200 COLOUR 1 WIDTH 5
num=18:IF count<18 THEN num=count
FOR loop=1 TO num
  PRINT AT (54;loop);loop;ob$(loop)
  IF loop+18<=count THEN PRINT AT (66;loop);loop+18;ob$(loop+18)
NEXT loop
  PRINT AT (54;20);STRING$(24," ")
  PRINT AT (54;21);STRING$(24," ")
  PRINT AT (54;20);"Draw order?"
  FOR loop=1 TO count
    PRINT AT (54;21);loop;" Object Num:       "
    INPUT AT (69;21);order(loop)
    printrow=order(loop):printcol=55
    IF printrow>18 THEN printrow=printrow-18:printcol=67
    PRINT AT (printcol;printrow);"**"
  NEXT loop
RETURN
```

```
LABEL newsite
PRINT AT (54;20);"Click to locate"
status=-1
WHILE status=-1
  x=XMOUSE:y=YMOUSE*YPIXEL
  status=BUTTON(1)
  oblength=obsize(num,1)*4:obwidth=obsize(num,2)*2
  IF x<=0 OR x>=long-oblength OR y<=0 OR y>=wide-obwidth THEN status=-1
   REM reject attempts to display off plan area
WEND
x(1)=x:y(1)=y
x(2)=x:y(2)=y+obwidth
x(3)=x+oblength:y(3)=y+obwidth
x(4)=x+oblength:y(4)=y
RETURN

LABEL sited
FOR loop=1 TO 4
  x(loop)=(obx(num,loop)+midx)*4
  y(loop)=oby(num,loop)*2
NEXT loop
RETURN

LABEL moveit
GOSUB drawit
FOR copy=1 TO 4
  a(copy)=x(copy)
  b(copy)=y(copy)
NEXT copy
xmove=x-x(1):ymove=y-y(1)
FOR loop=1 TO 4
  x(loop)=x(loop)+xmove
  y(loop)=y(loop)+ymove
NEXT loop
GOSUB check
WHILE BUTTON(1)=0:WEND
RETURN

LABEL rotate
rotated=rotated+1
GOSUB drawit
x1=(x(1)+x(3))/2
y1=(y(1)+y(3))/2
```

```
  REM find mid-point - this is the centre of rotation
cosangle=COS(15):sinangle=SIN(15)
FOR n=1 TO 4
   REM take copies in case of problems
   a(n)=x(n)
   b(n)=y(n)
   REM scale down before rotation
   x(n)=(x(n)-x1)/4
   y(n)=(y(n)-y1)/2
   temp=x(n)*cosangle+y(n)*sinangle
   y(n)=y(n)*cosangle-x(n)*sinangle
   REM scale up afterwards
   x(n)=temp*4+x1
   y(n)=y(n)*2+y1
NEXT n
GOSUB check:IF flag=1 THEN rotated=rotated-1
IF rotated<6 THEN RETURN
REM switch corners round so that 1 remains at bottom left
tempx=x(4):tempy=y(4)
FOR loop=4 TO 2 STEP -1
  x(loop)=x(loop-1)
  y(loop)=y(loop-1)
NEXT loop
x(1)=tempx
y(1)=tempy
rotated=0
RETURN

LABEL drawit
GRAPHICS MODE 3
LINE x(1);y(1),x(2);y(2),x(3);y(3),x(4);y(4),x(1);y(1)
RETURN

LABEL check
GRAPHICS MODE 1
flag=0
FOR n=1 TO 4
   REM check that rotated object will fit in room
   IF x(n)<=0 OR x(n)>=long OR y(n)<=0 OR y(n)>=wide THEN   flag=1
NEXT n
IF flag=0 THEN RETURN
```

```
REM restore original co-ordinates
FOR copy=1 TO 4
  x(copy)=a(copy)
  y(copy)=b(copy)
NEXT copy
RETURN


LABEL view
CLS
nearflag=0
 REM Floor
FOR n=1 TO 4
   REM scale for viewing
  x(n)=(rmx(n)+midx)*6.4
  z(n)=(rmz(n)+midz)*3.2
NEXT n
col=floorcol:pat=floorpat:GOSUB drawshape


REM Walls
FOR side=1 TO 3
  FOR corner=1 TO 4
     REM get corner reference number
    ref=roomside(side,corner)
     REM scale for viewing
    x(corner)=(rmx(ref)+midx)*6.4
    z(corner)=(rmz(ref)+midz)*3.2
  NEXT corner
  col=wallcol(side):pat=wallpat(side):GOSUB drawshape
NEXT side


REM Ceiling
FOR n=1 TO 4
  x(n)=(rmx(n+4)+midx)*6.4
  z(n)=(rmz(n+4)+midz)*3.2
NEXT n
col=ceilingcol:pat=ceilingpat:GOSUB drawshape


REM objects
FOR object=1 TO count
  n=order(object)
  col=obcol(n):pat=obpat(n)
  face(1)=1
  face(2)=0
  IF oby(n,2)>oby(n,3)+0.1 THEN face(2)=3 ELSE IF obx(n,3)<0 THEN face(2)=3
    ELSE IF obx(n,1)>0 THEN face(2)=2
```

```
   face(3)=0
   IF obz(n,5)<0 THEN face(3)=5 ELSE IF obz(n,1)>0 THEN face(3)=4
   GOSUB faces
NEXT object
GOSUB anykey
RETURN


LABEL faces
FOR num=1 TO 3
   IF face(num)=0 THEN GOTO nextface
   RESTORE facedata
   readit=0
   WHILE readit<(face(num)-1)*4
     READ dummy
     readit=readit+1
   WEND
   FOR c=1 TO 4
     READ corner
     pers=per^(oby(n,corner)/100)
     x(c)=(obx(n,corner)*pers+midx)*6.4
     z(c)=(obz(n,corner)*pers+midz)*3.2
   NEXT c
   nearflag=0:IF oby(n,1)<5 THEN nearflag=1
     REM nearflag set if object close to viewing side
   GOSUB drawshape

   LABEL nextface
NEXT num
RETURN


LABEL facedata
DATA 1,5,8,4,1,2,6,5,3,4,8,7,1,2,3,4,5,6,7,8

LABEL drawshape
FOR coord=1 TO 4
   REM check for off screen
   IF x(coord)<0 THEN x(coord)=0
   IF x(coord)>639 THEN x(coord)=639
   IF z(coord)<0 THEN z(coord)=0
   IF z(coord)>199 THEN z(coord)=199
NEXT coord

IF nearflag=0 THEN SHAPE x(1);z(1),x(2);z(2),x(3);z(3),x(4);z(4),x(1);z(1)
   COLOUR col FILL WITH pat
LINE x(1);z(1),x(2);z(2),x(3);z(3),x(4);z(4),x(1);z(1) COLOUR 1
RETURN
```

```
LABEL change
PRINT AT (5;21);"Room is being rotated through 90 degrees"
oldmidx=midx
SWAP roomlength,roomwidth
GOSUB setroom
tempcol=wallcol(4):temppat=wallpat(4)
FOR side=4 TO 2 STEP -1
  wallcol(side)=wallcol(side-1)
  wallpat(side)=wallpat(side-1)
NEXT side
wallcol(1)=tempcol:wallpat(1)=temppat
IF count=0 THEN RETURN
FOR loop=1 TO count
  SWAP obsize(loop,1),obsize(loop,2)
  tempx=obx(loop,4)
  tempy=oby(loop,4)
  FOR corner=4 TO 2 STEP -1
    obx(loop,corner)=oby(loop,corner-1)-midx:
    oby(loop,corner)=oldmidx-obx(loop,corner-1)
  NEXT corner
  obx(loop,1)=tempy-midx
  oby(loop,1)=oldmidx-tempx
  tempx=obx(loop,8)
  tempy=oby(loop,8)
  FOR corner=8 TO 6 STEP -1
    obx(loop,corner)=oby(loop,corner-1)-midx
    oby(loop,corner)=oldmidx-obx(loop,corner-1)
  NEXT corner
  obx(loop,5)=tempy-midx:oby(loop,5)=oldmidx-tempx
NEXT loop
RETURN

LABEL saver
PRINT AT (5;21);"Filename for saving:_____"
INPUT AT (25;21);file$
IF LEN(file$)>8 THEN file$=LEFT$(file$,8)
WHILE LEN(file$)<8:file$=file$+" ":WEND
file$=UPPER$(file$)+".RMP"
PRINT AT (5;21);"Saving room plan ";file$;". Please wait."
OPEN #5 OUTPUT file$
PRINT #5,roomlength,roomwidth,roomheight,floorcol,floorpat
FOR sides=1 TO 4
  FOR corner=1 TO 4
    PRINT #5,roomside(side,corner)
  NEXT corner
NEXT side
```

```
FOR side=1 TO 4
  PRINT #5,wallcol(side),wallpat(side)
NEXT side
PRINT #5,ceilingcol,ceilingpat
PRINT #5,count
FOR loop=1 TO count
  PRINT #5,ob$(loop)
  FOR corner=1 TO 8
    PRINT #5,obx(loop,corner),oby(loop,corner),obz(loop,corner)
  NEXT corner
  PRINT #5,obcol(loop),obpat(loop),order(loop)
  FOR side=1 TO 4
    PRINT #5,obsize(loop,side)
  NEXT side
NEXT loop
CLOSE #5
RETURN


LABEL loader
PRINT AT (5;21);"Filename for loading:_____"
INPUT AT (25;21);file$
IF LEN(file$)>8 THEN file$=LEFT$(file$,8)
WHILE LEN(file$)<8:file$=file$+" ":WEND
file$=UPPER$(file$)+".RMP"
x$=FIND$(file$):IF x$<>file$ THEN PRINT "Not found":GOSUB anykey:RETURN
PRINT AT(5;21);"Loading room plan ";file$;". Please wait."
OPEN #5 INPUT file$
INPUT #5,roomlength,roomwidth,roomheight,floorcol,floorpat
FOR side=1 TO 4
  FOR corner=1 TO 4
    INPUT #5,roomside(side,corner)
  NEXT corner
NEXT side
FOR side=1 TO 4
  INPUT #5,wallcol(side),wallpat(side)
NEXT side
INPUT #5,ceilingcol,ceilingpat
INPUT #5,count
FOR loop=1 TO count
  INPUT #5,ob$(loop)
  FOR corner=1 TO 8
    INPUT #5,obx(loop,corner),oby(loop,corner),obz(loop,corner)
  NEXT corner
  INPUT #5,obcol(loop),obpat(loop),order(loop)
  FOR side=1 TO 4
    INPUT #5,obsize(loop,side)
```

```
   NEXT side
NEXT loop
CLOSE #5
GOSUB setroom
RETURN

LABEL anykey
PRINT AT (2;21);"Press any key to continue"
ky$=""
WHILE ky$="":ky$=INKEY$:WEND
RETURN

LABEL exit
exit=1
RETURN
```

PART 4

RANDOM-ACCESS FILES

Chapter 12

Club Membership

This program serves as an introduction to random-access file handling, and also offers a simple system for organising the membership records of a club. For each member it stores their name, address and phone number, as well as the renewal month for subscriptions, whether or not these have been paid, the category of membership and a list of teams to which they belong. The program will output details of any individual, and lists of all members, sorted into category or not, lists of those whose subscriptions are due, and the members of any specified team.

It must be stated that if you do intend to use this program for organising a club, then you will fall within the orbit of the Data Protection Act. In essence, this requires that you should register with the Data Protection Registrar, seek the permission of members to store their records on computer and ensure the security of the files. There are exemptions for some categories of data user, but do check with the Data Protection Registrar before going ahead with any computerisation.

Program structure

Initialisation

Set screen
Define record structures
Set up months array
Get file/set up new one if needed

Main loop

Display options
Perform options
Until exit selected

Options

Add new member	*add*
Get details	
Find ref number and save	
Repeat if wanted	

Display single record	*show*
Which ref number?	*getnum*
Show details on screen	
Repeat if wanted	

Update record	*updater*
Which ref number?	*getnum*
Each field in turn, change if required	*change*
Repeat if wanted	

Remove member from list	*remove*
Which ref number?	*getnum*
Put blanks in record	
Note record number for re-use later	

Print full list	*all*
Get output stream	*outwhere*
Print headings	
For all current members	*printout*
Format details and print	
Close stream if disk output	

Print list sorted by membership category	*sorted*
Get sorting flag	
Get output stream, print headings and	
List committee members	*all*
List ordinary, then junior members	*printout*

Show subscriptions due	*subdue*
Get output stream	*outwhere*
Print heading	
For all members	
Compare month with renewal month	

```
        Check paid flag
        Print name and tel.no. if not paid
     Print team list                               team
        Get output stream                          outwhere
        Get team name to look for
        For all members
           Check team against given team name
           Print name and tel.no. of team member

  Exit
     Store list of re-usable record numbers
     Store number of members
     Close file
```

Key subroutines

```
  Get record number                                getnum
     If not known, get name & check file           findmem

  Get output stream                                outwhere
     Screen, paper or disk
     If disk, get filename and open stream
```

Notes

Random and sequential files

In a sequential file, data is stored in a continual stream, so that the only way to access the umpteenth record is to read through umpteen minus one to get there. If you need to alter the contents of the file, you must either read the whole lot into memory, make changes and write it all out again, or create a new version of the file and transfer the records over to it one at a time, making alterations as needed.

With a random-access file, each record occupies an identifiable place on the disk and so may be accessed individually. While this means that you do not have to use either internal memory or a second file to update a file, it also means that every read or write operation requires another disk access.

Where the total quantity of data in a file is relatively small — no more than 30 or 40K, then the most satisfactory solution is usually to use a simple sequential file and internal storage. The whole file can then be read into an array, or set of arrays, at the start of the program, and written back to disk at the end. It takes very little time to transfer that much data to and from disk, and once in memory, the arrays can be updated, searched and sorted very conveniently.

Where there is much more data, or where the Basic program is itself so vast that it leaves only negligible memory for arrays, a random file should normally be used. Updating a sequential file by transferring corrected records to a new file is a pain to program, and in practice, is generally slower than using a random file system.

In a random file, data is grouped into records and subdivided into fields, according to a structure which will have been defined early in the program. A record may contain any number of different types of variables, and may be of any size. The only limitation is that which applies to all Basic2 lines — you can't use more than 255 characters. So, as long as the names used for the variables, or fields, are kept as short as possible, the record may contain a dozen or more fields.

When Basic2 transfers the record to disk, the data in the fields — whatever their type — is packed into a single string, with each field in its own assigned place. Within the program, however, the fields behave exactly like simple variables and may be PRINTed, INPUT and evaluated in the normal way. (Note though, that to assign a value to a field within such a record string, the string must exist already. Either GET it, or fill it with spaces, before you start to use it.)

Before turning to the first program, it may be useful to work through a simple example. Take a program that starts:

```
RECORD member;name$ FIXED 20,age BYTE,type$ FIXED 1,rating WORD
OPEN #5 RANDOM "clublist" LENGTH 24
```

All string variables must be of fixed length — how long depends upon the number of characters you need. Number variables must be of a defined type so that Basic2 knows how much space to assign to them within the packed string; BYTEs take one character, WORDs take two. The overall length of the record is therefore

$$20 + 1 + 1 + 2 = 24$$

The LENGTH part of the OPEN line may be omitted, but if it is Basic2 will allocate a length of 128 characters. In this case it would lead to very inefficient use of disk space.

```
GET #5, club$ AT 4
PRINT club$.member.name$
IF club$.member.age<18 THEN PRINT "Junior" ELSE PRINT "Adult"
```

When the record for Fred Wilson, who is 42 and a Committee member with a rating of 8574, is read into *club$*, the resulting string would look like this:

```
Fred Wilson    *C!^
```

The 21st character of the packed string is an asterisk (ASCII 42), which represents his age; *club$. member. age* has the value 42. The 23rd and 24th characters have ASCII codes of 33 and 126, giving a WORD value of 33*256 + 126 = 8574. Although the *name$* field occupies 20 characters, the variable *club$.member.name$* has a length of only 11 as trailing spaces are ignored.

The same random file may contain records with different structures as long as the file LENGTH is high enough to accommodate the longest type of record. Basic doesn't mind. It is a string that you GET from or PUT onto disk; how it is unpacked within the program is up to you. You will find two record definitions used in the Membership program. The first, *member* is the structure used for the membership details; the second *master*, sets up a string in which to store the membership numbers which may be re-used, and a single WORD variable to keep a count of the numbers of members. The first record on the file has the *master* structure; all the rest are *members*.

```
RECORD member;name$ FIXED 30,add$ FIXED 50,tel$ FIXED 12,
  - category$ FIXED 1,month UBYTE,paid$ FIXED 1,team$ FIXED 20
RECORD master;spare$ FIXED 100,number UWORD
```

Re-using records for disk efficiency

The way that record numbers can be re-used is worth a closer look. With a random file, each record is occupies a distinct space on the disk. As the file grows, so more space is taken up. Thus 10 records, each of 100 bytes will require 1000 bytes of disk space. If this was a sequential file and you deleted a record, then the new version of the file would only take 900 bytes. With a random file, the space is not released when a record is no longer required − its slot is still there, though it may be filled with blanks. The three files developed in this section all re-use the slots vacated by deleted records, and so economise on disk space. This should prove particularly valuable in estate agency and similar systems where there may be a high turnover of records.

When a record is deleted, its space is filled with blanks, and the record number is stored, as an ASCII character, in the *reuse$* variable − later written to disk in the *master.spare$* form. When a record is added to the file, the program will first check *reuse$* to see if there are any numbers there, and use any spare slot that it finds; if not, the new record will be added to the end of the file:

```
IF LEN$(reuse$)>0 THEN memnum=ASC(LEFT$(reuse$,1)):reuse$=MID$(reuse$,2)
  ELSE num=num+1:memnum=num
```

Conversion to keyed form

If you want to be able to access the records in alphabetical order, then the best solution is to convert the program so that it uses a KEYed file, rather than the simpler random form. With a keyed file, Basic2 maintains an index of the data in whichever fields are selected as KEYs. The fields used may be any type of number variables, or string variables, FIXED or not, of no more than 30 characters.

Assuming that only a single KEY will be needed, on the name, these are that alterations that will be needed:

1   When the file is OPENed, you must specify the name of the file in which the *index* is to be stored:

```
OPEN #5 RANDOM list$ INDEX index$ LENGTH 116
```

2   The index must then be defined, giving its stream, identification number and variable type. The KEY field here is *name$*, a fixed-length string. When the UNIQUE switch is ON, the data written into the key field of each record must be different. Leaving it OFF allows the membership system to cope with two John Smiths!:

```
KEYSPEC #5 INDEX 1 FIXED 30 UNIQUE OFF
```

3   Records are written to the file with **ADDREC**, rather than the normal **PUT**; and note that the KEY field must be specified. Where there are two or more KEYs, the command must end with **INDEX** *number*:

```
ADDREC #5, club$ KEY name$
```

4   To read through the file in name order, you should then use the **POSITION** command, first with the **INDEX** option to point to the start of the index, then with **NEXT** to move on to the subsequent record:

```
POSITION #5, club$ INDEX 1
   WHILE NOT EOF(#5)
      GET #5,club$
      ....(format and print)
      POSITION #5 NEXT
   WEND
```

5   An individual record can be found directly, without hunting through the file, by specifying the key data in a POSITION command. Follow this with a GET line to read the record:

```
INPUT "Name to find ";member_name$
POSITION #5 KEY member_name$
GET #5, club$
```

6   GET can be used as a function to check that a particular record is there — *found* will be 0 if it is. Use it before trying to read the record to avoid an error:

```
INPUT "Name to find ";member_name$
found=GET #5,club$ KEY member_name$
IF found<>0 THEN PRINT "No such member"
POSITION #5 KEY member_name$
```

The membership program

```
REM club records

DRIVE "B"

SCREEN #1 TEXT 80 FIXED,25 FIXED
WINDOW # 1 FULL ON
WINDOW TITLE "CLUB RECORDS"

RECORD member;name$ FIXED 30,add$ FIXED 50,tel$ FIXED 12,category$ FIXED 1,
- month UBYTE,paid$ FIXED 1,team$ FIXED 20
RECORD master;spare$ FIXED 100,number UWORD
blank$=STRING$(116," ")

DIM month$(12)
RESTORE
FOR m=1 TO 12:READ month$(m):NEXT m
DATA January,February,March,April,May,June,July,August,September,October,
 - November,December
thismonth=VAL(MID$(DATE$,4,2))

LABEL begin
found=0:newlist=0
WHILE found=0
  INPUT "Name of list? ";list$
  list$=list$ "          "
  list$=UPPER$(LEFT$(list$,8))+".CLB"
  x$=FIND$(list$):IF x$=list$ THEN found=1
  IF found=0 THEN GOSUB checkname
WEND

OPEN #5 RANDOM list$ LENGTH 116
club$=blank$
check$=blank$
IF newlist THEN num=1:reuse$="":GOTO menu
GET #5,check$ AT 1
num=check$.master.number
reuse$=check$.master.spare$
```

```
IF newlist=0 THEN PRINT num-1;" members recorded."
GOSUB anykey

LABEL menu
REPEAT
  CLS
  sorting=0
  PRINT AT (20;2);"ADD NEW MEMBER .....................1"
  PRINT AT (20;4);"DISPLAY MEMBER'S RECORD.............2"
  PRINT AT (20;6);"UPDATE MEMBER'S RECORD..............3"
  PRINT AT (20;8);"REMOVE MEMBER.......................4"
  PRINT AT (20;10);"FULL MEMBERSHIP LIST................5"
  PRINT AT (20;12);"SORTED MEMBERSHIP LIST..............6"
  PRINT AT (20;14);"SUBSCRIPTIONS DUE...................7"
  PRINT AT (20;16);"TEAM LISTS..........................8"
  PRINT AT (20;18);"EXIT FROM PROGRAM...................9"

  REPEAT
    opt$=UPPER$(INKEY$)
  UNTIL opt$>="1" AND opt$<="9"
  opt=VAL(opt$)
  ON opt GOSUB add,show,updater,remove,all,sorted,subdue,team,exit
UNTIL opt$="9"

END

LABEL checkname
PRINT "List ";list$;" not found."
INPUT "Start new list (Y/N) ";a$
IF UPPER$(a$)="Y" THEN found=1:newlist=1
RETURN

LABEL add
REPEAT
  CLS
  WINDOW CURSOR ON
  PRINT "New Member's Details"
  INPUT "Name ";a$
  club$.member.name$=UPPER$(a$)
  LINE INPUT "Address ";a$
    REM line input allows commas in address
  club$.member.add$=UPPER$(a$)
  INPUT "Telephone Number ";club$.member.tel$
  PRINT "Membership status:"
  PRINT "      Committee Member......C"
  PRINT "      Ordinary Member.......O"
```

```
  PRINT "     Junior Member.........J"
  INPUT "O/C/J ";a$
  club$.member.category$=UPPER$(a$)
  PRINT "Renewal month ";month$(thismonth)
  INPUT "Accept (Y/N) ";a$
  IF UPPER$(a$)="Y" THEN club$.member.month=thismonth ELSE INPUT
 - "Renewal month number (1 to 12) ";club$.member.month
  INPUT "Dues Paid for this year (Y/N) ";a$
  club$.member.paid$=UPPER$(a$)
  INPUT "Team memberships ";a$
  club$.member.team$=UPPER$(a$)
  IF LEN$(reuse$)>0 THEN memnum=ASC(LEFT$(reuse$,1)):reuse$=MID$(reuse$,2)
   - ELSE num=num+1:memnum=num
  PUT #5,club$ AT memnum
  PRINT "Membership number is ";memnum
  INPUT "Another new member (Y/N)";a$
UNTIL a$="n" OR a$="N"
WINDOW CURSOR OFF
RETURN


LABEL show
REPEAT
  GOSUB getnum:IF memnum=0 THEN GOTO showexit
  PRINT "Address: ";club$.member.add$
  PRINT "Tel. No.:";club$.member.tel$
  c$=club$.member.category$
  cat$="Ordinary"
  IF c$="C" THEN cat$="Committee" ELSE IF c$="J" THEN cat$="Junior"
  PRINT "Category:";cat$;" Member"
  PRINT "Renewal in ";month$(club$.member.month)
  p$=club$.member.paid$
  IF p$="Y" THEN paid$=" Paid" ELSE paid$=" Due"
  PRINT "Subscription ";paid$
  PRINT "Teams:     ";club$.member.team$

  LABEL showexit
  INPUT "Another Member?";a$
UNTIL a$="n" OR a$="N"
RETURN

LABEL updater
REPEAT
  number=0
  GOSUB getnum
  IF memnum=0 THEN GOTO upexit
  GOSUB change
```

```
   IF a$="Y" THEN club$.member.name$=UPPER$(new$)
   PRINT "Address: ";club$.member.add$
   GOSUB change
   IF a$="Y" THEN club$.member.add$=UPPER$(new$)
   PRINT "Tel. No.:";club$.member.tel$
   GOSUB change
   IF a$="Y" THEN club$.member.tel$=UPPER$(new$)
   c$=club$.member.category$
   cat$="Ordinary"
   IF c$="C" THEN cat$="Committee" ELSE IF c$="J" THEN cat$="Junior"
   PRINT "Category:";cat$;" Member"
   GOSUB change
   IF a$="Y" THEN club$.member.category$=UPPER$(new$)
   PRINT "Renewal in ";month$(club$.member.month)
   number=1:GOSUB change
   IF a$="Y" THEN club$.member.month=VAL(new$)
   p$=club$.member.paid$
   IF p$="Y" THEN paid$=" Paid" ELSE paid$=" Due"
   PRINT "Subscription ";p$;" indicates ";paid$
   number=0:GOSUB change
   IF a$="Y" THEN club$.member.paid$=UPPER$(new$)
   PRINT "Teams:      ";club$.member.team$
   GOSUB change
   IF a$="Y" THEN club$.member.team$=UPPER$(new$)
   PUT #5,club$ AT memnum

  LABEL upexit
  INPUT "Another Member?";a$
UNTIL a$="n" OR a$="N"
RETURN

LABEL change
INPUT "Change this (Y/N) ";a$
a$=UPPER$(a$)
IF a$="N" THEN RETURN
LABEL getdata
WINDOW CURSOR ON
LINE INPUT "New data for this field ";new$
IF number AND LEFT$(new$,1)>"9" THEN PRINT "Number please!":GOTO getdata
WINDOW CURSOR OFF
RETURN

LABEL remove
REPEAT
  CLS
  GOSUB getnum
```

```
    IF memnum=0 THEN GOTO reexit
    INPUT "Really delete this name (Y/N) ";a$
    IF UPPER$(a$)="N" THEN GOTO reexit
    reuse$=reuse$+CHR$(memnum)
    PUT #5,blank$ AT memnum
    LABEL reexit
    INPUT "Another Member?";a$
UNTIL a$="n" OR a$="N"
RETURN


LABEL getnum
CLS
INPUT "Membership number? (0 if not known)";memnum
IF memnum=0 THEN GOSUB findmem
IF memnum=0 THEN RETURN
GET #5,club$ AT memnum
PRINT "Name:    ";club$.member.name$
RETURN


LABEL findmem
WINDOW CURSOR ON
INPUT "Member's name?";name$
FOR n=2 TO num
  GET #5,club$ AT n
  temp$=club$.member.name$
  IF INSTR(temp$,UPPER$(name$)) =0 THEN GOTO nextmember
  PRINT temp$;" Number ";n
  INPUT "Is this the one (Y/N) ";a$
  IF UPPER$(a$)="Y" THEN memnum=n:n=num

  LABEL nextmember
NEXT n
IF memnum=0 THEN PRINT "No such member. "
WINDOW CURSOR OFF
RETURN


LABEL all
GOSUB outwhere
PRINT #where,"  Membership List for ";LEFT$(list$,8);" club"
PRINT #where
PRINT #where,"    Name           Telephone Subscription   Category      Teams"

LABEL printout
IF sorting THEN PRINT #where,"    ";cat$" MEMBERS"
FOR ptr=2 TO num
  GET #5,club$ AT ptr
```

```
    IF sorting AND club$.member.category$<>c$ THEN GOTO nextpointer
    IF club$=blank$ THEN GOTO nextpointer
    out$=STR$(ptr)
    name$=club$.member.name$
    long=LEN(name$)
    newname$=" "
    find=INSTR(name$," ")
     REM routine to turn forenames into initials
    WHILE find>0
      newname$=newname$+LEFT$(name$,1)+"."
      long=long-find
      name$=RIGHT$(name$,long)
      find=INSTR(name$," ")
    WEND
    newname$=newname$+name$
    out$=out$+newname$
    WHILE LEN(out$)<16:out$=out$+" ":WEND
    out$=out$+club$.member.tel$
    WHILE LEN(out$)<30:out$=out$+" ":WEND
    renewmonth$=month$(club$.member.month)
    out$=out$+renewmonth$
    WHILE LEN(out$)<40:out$=out$+" ":WEND
    p$=club$.member.paid$
    IF p$="Y" THEN paid$="Paid" ELSE paid$="Due "
    out$=out$+paid$+"      "
    IF NOT(sorting) THEN out$=out$+club$.member.category$
    out$=out$+"        "+club$.member.team$
    PRINT #where,out$

    LABEL nextpointer
  NEXT ptr
  PRINT #where
  IF sorting AND c$<>"J" THEN RETURN
  GOSUB anykey
  IF where=6 THEN CLOSE #6
  RETURN

  LABEL sorted
  sorting=1
  c$="C":cat$="COMMITTEE":GOSUB all
  c$="O":cat$="ORDINARY":GOSUB printout
  c$="J":cat$="JUNIOR":GOSUB printout
  RETURN

  LABEL subdue
  GOSUB outwhere
```

```
PRINT #where,"Renewals due in or before ";month$(thismonth)
FOR ptr=2 TO num
  GET #5,club$ AT ptr
  month=club$.member.month
  paid$=club$.member.paid$
  IF month<=thismonth AND paid$="N" THEN PRINT #where,club$.member.name$
NEXT ptr
GOSUB anykey
IF where=6 THEN CLOSE #6
RETURN


LABEL team
WINDOW CURSOR ON
CLS
GOSUB outwhere
INPUT "Team to look for? ";t$
PRINT #where," Members who belong to ";t$;" team"
WINDOW CURSOR OFF
FOR ptr=2 TO num
  GET #5,club$ AT ptr
  find=INSTR(club$.member.team$,UPPER$(t$))
  IF find THEN PRINT #where,club$.member.name$;"Tel. No.";club$.member.tel$
NEXT ptr
GOSUB anykey
IF where=6 THEN CLOSE #6
RETURN


LABEL outwhere
CLS
REPEAT
  INPUT "Output to screen, paper or disk? (S/P/D) ";a$
  a$=UPPER$(a$)
UNTIL a$="S" OR a$="P" OR a$="D"
IF a$="S" THEN where=1:RETURN
IF a$="P" THEN where=0:RETURN
where=6
INPUT "Filename for this report ";filerep$
filerep$=UPPER$(LEFT$(filerep$,8))+".REP"
OPEN #6 OUTPUT filerep$
RETURN


LABEL exit
check$.master.spare$=reuse$
check$.master.number=num
PUT #5,check$ AT 1
CLOSE #5
```

```
exit=1
RETURN

LABEL anykey
PRINT AT (1;21);"Press any key to go on"
WHILE ky$<>"":ky$=INKEY$:WEND
WHILE ky$="":ky$=INKEY$:WEND
RETURN
```

Chapter 13

Payroll Processing

This program could be used to process the payroll for weekly paid employees in a small or medium-sized business, where wages are paid in cash. It will calculate gross wages, tax, National Insurance and pensions contributions; print out the payslips and a coin and note analysis, and maintain Year-To-Date totals for individual workers and for the firm as a whole. It does have some distinct limitations when compared with commercially available payroll software. It cannot handle Sick Pay, P45s, P60s and other forms, and uses only the 'time-and-a-half' overtime rate. Neither does it write the cheques or giros as an alternative to cash payments, nor perform the departmental analysis which would be needed in larger businesses. All of these could be added, if wanted, without too much trouble.

The comments made in the previous chapter about registration under the Data Protection Act apply with even more force here. If any personal details about employees — and that definitely includes wages — are kept on computer, you must register. It is not sufficient to use works numbers, rather than names, in the payroll file as the list of numbers and names (which must exist) allows the computerised data to be related to individuals. Registration may be a bit of a chore, but computerisation can make significant inroads into the clerical workload and should more than offset the bother, and the minor costs, of registration.

Program structure

Initialisation

Record structure
National Insurance and tax rates
Coin and note arrays

Look for COMPANY.PAY file; if not present
   Get initial data about company
Read company data from file into variables

Main loop

Display options
Perform selected option
Until exit

Options

Add new employee	*add*
Get details:	
Name, hourly rate, normal working hours,	
Tax code, Y-T-D totals	
Add to file	

Add new employee   *add*
  Get details:
    Name, hourly rate, normal working hours,
    Tax code, Y-T-D totals
  Add to file

Display employee's record   *show*
  Get ref number   *getnum*
  Display details with field headings

Employee leaves   *leave*
  Get ref number   *getnum*
  Check before deletion
  Mark hourly rate to 0 as flag to show left employ

List all employees   *listall*
  Get output stream   *outwhere*
  Print headings
  For all employees
    Print name and number
    If left firm, display appropriate message
  If output to disk, close stream

Calculate wages and print slips   *payrun*
  Get output stream for payslips   *outwhere*
  For each current employee
    Check hourly rate
      Get new if changed
    Check hours worked
      Get hours if not standard week
    Calculate in turn and add to Y-T-D totals
      Gross

      Pension
      National Insurance
      Tax
      Net
    Do coin and note analysis for wage packet
      Add to totals
      Print payslip

Show weekly totals   *totals*
    Get output stream   *outwhere*
    Print current totals for firm
    Print coin and note requirements for wages

Exit and closedown   *exit*
    Store updated company totals on disk

Notes

You may well notice some distinct similarities between parts of this program and the earlier Membership program. This is no accident. Having planned the payroll program and worked out what routines would be needed, MEMBERS was copied, the relevant parts identified and the remainder cut out. One of the great advantages of structured programming is that it is very easy to re-use routines — there's never any point in writing the same thing twice.

File structure

There is only a single RECORD definition in this program, but it is used in two different ways. Most of the records in the file store the relevant details for the employees — and their nature should be obvious from the fieldnames in the definition:

```
RECORD emp;name$ FIXED 30,rate,hours,taxcode WORD,gross,pension,ni,tax,net
```

The first record of the file holds the data for the company, with the fields being used as shown in Table 13.1.

There has been no attempt here to optimise disk space by re-using the records of employees who have left. This should not be done as it is important for accountancy purposes to maintain records of all employees for the whole financial year, whether they leave during that time or not. When a person does leave, the *rate* field in their record is set to 0. An alternative worth considering, especially if you wish to retain the

TABLE 13.1

Field name	Data
name$	Company name
rate	Number of employees
hours	Standard working hours
taxcode	Week number (needed for tax calculations)
gross, etc	Y-T-D totals for the whole company

pay rate for future reference, is to set up a special field to record leaving. This may contain a simple 0/1 flag, or may hold the week number of their last employment.

National Insurance calculations

At the start of the program, the National Insurance band limits and rates are assigned to the arrays *band()* and *ni()*, and it is assumed that all employees are contracted in. At the time of writing, those earning less than £38 a week pay no National Insurance contributions; those with weekly wages of up to £60 are charged at 5%; up to £90 at 7%; and any up to the maximum of £285 at 9%. The High Band charges have been ignored in this program:

```
band(1)=38:ni(1)=.0
band(2)=60:ni(2)=.05
band(3)=95:ni(3)=.07
band(4)=285:ni(4)=.09
```

Someone earning £90 would therefore pay at the 7% rate − £6.30 − while a higher paid colleague, at £100, would pay £9.00. The value can be calculated quite easily by looping through the band limits, with a further check for the higher paid workers:

```
FOR level=1 TO 4
   IF gross<=band(level) THEN ni=gross*ni(level):level=4
NEXT level
IF gross>band(4) THEN ni=band(4)*ni(4)
```

Thus, a £90 gross wage would pass through the loop twice before being trapped by the test on the third time. A wage of £300 would fail the test at each level, but be caught by the subsequent line.

Tax calculations

These are rather more complex to handle, as the total tax for an individual will depend upon his or her tax code, and may consist of several percentages at different levels. The tax band data is set up to suit the way that the calculations are managed later on. At the time of writing, the Basic Rate tax band runs up to £17,900 p.a., or £344.23 per week; the next £2,500 p.a., or £48.07 per week is taxed at 40%; the next £5,000 p.a. (£96.15 per week) at 45% and so on:

```
tband(1)=344.23:trate(1)=.27
tband(2)=48.07:trate(2)=.4
tband(3)=96.15:trate(3)=.45
tband(4)=151.92:trate(4)=.5
tband(5)=151.92:trate(5)=.55
trate(6)=.6
```

The employee's tax code will be in the form '520H', indicating total tax-free allowances of £5200 per year, which would translate to £100 tax-free per week. However, this only applies where the person has been in regular employment since the start of the tax year. Tax must be assessed on a Year-To-Date basis. So, if that person with the 520H tax code did not start work until part way through the year, or had been

TABLE 13.2

Week no.	Y-T-D tax-free	Wages	Y-T-D wages	Tax	Y-T-D tax	
1	100	0	0	0	0	
2	200	0	0	0	0	
3	300	0	0	0	0	
4	400	240	240	0	0	
5	500	200	440	0	0	
6	600	220	660	16.20	16.20	(27%60)
7	700	140	800	10.80	27.00	(+27%40)
8	800	0	800	-27.00	0	

in low-paid work until then, no tax would be due until the total earnings had accumulated to a level above the Year-To-Date allowances. In a similar way, if the person's tax code is changed during the year, or their earnings fall, there may be tax rebates due. An example of this is given in Table 13.2.

The first stage in calculating tax is therefore to find out how much could have been earned to date tax-free:

```
taxfree=(firm$.emp.taxcode*10)/52
taxfree=taxfree*wknum
```

Then the taxable pay to date is calculated by checking the current totals — note that the *gross* and *pension* values will include those from that week:

```
taxable=firm$.emp.gross-firm$.emp.pension-taxfree
```

The total tax due to date can then be calculated by finding the amount due at each level. You will see that the *taxable* amount is reduced by the band limit each time round the loop:

```
tax=0
FOR level=1 TO 5
   limit=tband(level)*wknum
  IF taxable<limit THEN tax=tax+taxable*trate(level):level=5
     ELSE tax=tax+limit*trate(level)
   taxable=taxable-limit
NEXT level
IF taxable>0 THEN tax=tax+taxable*trate(6)
```

At the end, *tax* represents the Year-To-Date tax due. The tax that has already been paid must be deducted from this to get the week's income tax. This can then be added into the Year-To-Date figures for the employee and for the firm:

```
tax=tax-firm$.emp.tax:REM deduct tax paid to date
tax=ROUND(tax,2)
firm$.emp.tax=firm$.emp.tax+tax
tottax=tottax+tax
```

Coin and note analysis

In essence this is a series of modulo divisions. At the start, the integer part of the *net* pay is taken off as pounds and the remainder is multiplied by 100 to convert the pence fraction to an integer.

With the *note()* array storing the denomination of the notes and the *pounds()* array recording how many will be needed for the total wage bill, this routine manages the £20, £10 and £5 notes:

```
poundcash=INT(net):pencecash=(net-poundcash)*100
FOR pay=1 TO 3
   temp=poundcash\note(pay)
```

```
    pounds(pay)=pounds(pay)+temp
    poundcash=poundcash MOD note(pay)
  NEXT pay
  pounds(4)=pounds(4)+poundcash
```

For example, with *poundcash* starting at 137, after the first trip round the loop, *pounds(1)* − the 20s − will have been increased by 6, i.e. 137/20, and *poundcash* reduced to 17. The second and third executions will give one each to the 10s and 5s; and at the end, the remaining 2 will be added to *pounds(4)* − the £1 coins.

A very similar routine performs the same function for the coins. (Note that in the actual program both routines include a couple of extra lines to record the individual employee's coin and note analysis on the payslip.)

The payroll program

```
REM payroll system

DRIVE "B"

SCREEN #1 TEXT 80 FIXED,25 FIXED
WINDOW # 1 FULL ON

RECORD emp;name$ FIXED 30,rate,hours,taxcode WORD,gross,pension,ni,tax,net

overtime_rate=1.5:REM all overtime paid at time and a half
pension_cont =0.04:REM pension contributions 4% of gross

  REM national insurance rates
band(1)=38:ni(1)=.0
band(2)=60:ni(2)=.05
band(3)=95:ni(3)=.07
band(4)=285:ni(4)=.09

  REM tax rate - weekly
tband(1)=344.23:trate(1)=.27
tband(2)=48.07:trate(2)=.4
tband(3)=96.15:trate(3)=.45
tband(4)=151.92:trate(4)=.5
tband(5)=151.92:trate(5)=.55
trate(6)=.6
```

```
 REM coin and note analysis
DIM pounds(4),note(4),pennies(6),coin(6)
note(1)=20:note(2)=10:note(3)=5:note(4)=1
coin(1)=50:coin(2)=20:coin(3)=10:coin(4)=5:coin(5)=2:coin(6)=1


LABEL begin
x$=FIND$("COMPANY .PAY")
IF x$="COMPANY .PAY" THEN OPEN #5 RANDOM "COMPANY.PAY" LENGTH 90:GOTO menu
PRINT "Payroll file not on this disk."
INPUT "Start new file or retry (S/R) ";a$
IF UPPER$(a$)="R" THEN GOTO begin


 REM start new file
OPEN #5 RANDOM "COMPANY.PAY" LENGTH 90
GET #5,firm$ AT 1
INPUT "Company name ";firm$.emp.name$
firm$.emp.rate=1:REM pointer for last record
INPUT "Normal working week ";firm$.emp.hours
INPUT "Tax year, week number ";wknum
firm$.emp.taxcode=wknum
IF wknum=1 THEN GOTO putdata
PRINT "Year to date totals"
INPUT "Gross pay ";firm$.emp.gross
INPUT "Pension contributions ";firm$.emp.pension
INPUT "National Insurance ";firm$.emp.ni
INPUT "Income tax ";firm$.emp.tax
INPUT "Net pay ";firm$.emp.net


LABEL putdata
PUT #5,firm$ AT 1



LABEL menu
GET #5,firm$ AT 1
company$=firm$.emp.name$
WINDOW TITLE company$+" Payroll"
num=firm$.emp.rate
standard=firm$.emp.hours
wknum=firm$.emp.taxcode
totgross=firm$.emp.gross
totpension=firm$.emp.pension
totni=firm$.emp.ni
tottax=firm$.emp.tax
totnet=firm$.emp.net


REPEAT
```

```
CLS
PRINT AT (20;2);"PERSONNEL RECORDS"
PRINT AT (20;4);"ADD NEW EMPLOYEE.....................1"
PRINT AT (20;6);"DISPLAY EMPLOYEE'S RECORD............2"
PRINT AT (20;8);"EMPLOYEE LEAVES.....................3"
PRINT AT (20;10);"LIST OF EMPLOYEES..................4"
PRINT AT (20;12);"PAYRUN"
PRINT AT (20;14);"CALCULATE WAGES.....................5"
PRINT AT (20;16);"WEEKLY TOTALS.......................6"
PRINT AT (20;18);"EXIT FROM PROGRAM...................7"
REPEAT
  opt$=INKEY$
UNTIL opt$>="1" AND opt$<="7"
opt=VAL(opt$)
ON opt GOSUB add,show,leave,listall,payrun,totals,exit
UNTIL opt$="7"

END

LABEL add
REPEAT
  CLS
  PRINT "New Employee's Details"
  INPUT "Name ";a$
  firm$.emp.name$=UPPER$(a$)
  INPUT "Hourly Rate";firm$.emp.rate
  INPUT "Standard week? (Y/N)";a$
  IF UPPER$(a$)="Y" THEN firm$.emp.hours=standard ELSE INPUT "Number of hours
  - in basic week ";firm$.emp.hours
  INPUT "Taxcode (Number only)";firm$.emp.taxcode
  IF wknum=0 THEN GOTO addexit
  PRINT "Year to date totals"
  INPUT "Gross Pay";firm$.emp.gross
  INPUT "Pension contributions";firm$.emp.pension
  INPUT "National Insurance";firm$.emp.ni
  INPUT "Income tax ";firm$.emp.tax
  INPUT "Net pay ";firm$.emp.net

  LABEL addexit
  num=num+1
  PUT #5,firm$ AT num
  PRINT "Work's reference number is ";num
  INPUT "Another new employee (Y/N)";a$
UNTIL a$="n" OR a$="N"
RETURN
```

181

```
LABEL show
REPEAT
  GOSUB getnum
  IF employee=0 THEN GOTO showexit
  PRINT "Reference Number ";employee
  PRINT "Hourly Rate ";firm$.emp.rate
  PRINT "Normal Working Week ";firm$.emp.hours
  PRINT "Tax Code ";firm$.emp.taxcode
  PRINT "Year to Date Totals "
  PRINT "Gross pay ";firm$.emp.gross
  PRINT "Pension Contributions ";firm$.emp.pension
  PRINT "National Insurance ";firm$.emp.ni
  PRINT "Income Tax ";firm$.emp.tax

  LABEL showexit
  INPUT "Another Employee (Y/N) ";a$
UNTIL a$="n" OR a$="N"
RETURN

LABEL leave
REPEAT
  CLS
  GOSUB getnum
  IF employee=0 THEN GOTO leaveout
  INPUT "Has this person really left (Y/N) ";a$
  IF UPPER$(a$)="N" THEN GOTO reexit
  firm$.emp.rate=0
  PUT #5,firm$ AT employee

  LABEL reexit
  INPUT "Another Employee (Y/N) ";a$
UNTIL a$="n" OR a$="N"
RETURN

LABEL getnum
CLS
INPUT "Reference Number? (0 if not known)";employee
IF employee=0 THEN GOSUB findnum
IF employee=0 THEN RETURN: REM not found by 'findnum'
GET #5,firm$ AT employee
PRINT "Name:    ";firm$.emp.name$
RETURN

LABEL findnum
INPUT "Employee's name?";name$
FOR enum=2 TO num
```

```
  GET #5,firm$ AT enum
  temp$=firm$.emp.name$
  IF INSTR(temp$,UPPER$(name$)) THEN GOSUB check
NEXT enum
IF employee=0 THEN PRINT "No such employee "
RETURN


LABEL check
PRINT temp$;" Number ";enum
INPUT "Is this the one (Y/N) ";a$
IF UPPER$(a$)="Y" THEN employee=enum:enum=num
RETURN


LABEL listall
GOSUB outwhere
PRINT #streamnum,company$;": Employees"
PRINT #streamnum
PRINT #streamnum,"     Name          Ref.No. "


LABEL printout
FOR worker=2 TO num
  GET #5,firm$ AT worker
  out$=firm$.emp.name$
  WHILE LEN(out$)<30:out$=out$+" ":WEND
  out$=out$+STR$(worker)
  IF firm$.emp.rate=0 THEN out$=out$+"  No longer on workforce"
  PRINT #streamnum,out$
NEXT worker
PRINT #streamnum
GOSUB anykey
IF streamnum=6 THEN CLOSE #6
RETURN


LABEL payrun
CLS
PRINT "WEEKLY PAYRUN ROUTINE"
PRINT "Week Number ";wknum
PRINT "Slips will be displayed on screen."
PRINT "Where do you want the second copy?"
GOSUB outwhere
FOR slip=2 TO num
  GET #5, firm$ AT slip
  IF firm$.emp.rate=0 THEN GOTO nextslip
  PRINT "Name ";firm$.emp.name$
  rate=firm$.emp.rate
  PRINT "Current rate ";rate
```

```
INPUT "New rate ? [RETURN] to leave ";a$
IF a$<>"" THEN rate=VAL(a$):firm$.emp.rate=rate
hours=firm$.emp.hours:overtime=0
PRINT "Hours worked ";hours
INPUT "Enter hours if different ";a$
IF a$<>"" THEN hr=VAL(a$):IF hr>hours THEN overtime=hr-hours ELSE hours=hr
 REM gross calculations
gross=hours*rate+overtime*overtime_rate*rate
gross=ROUND(gross,2)
firm$.emp.gross=firm$.emp.gross+gross
totgross=totgross+gross
 REM pension
pension=pension_cont*gross
pension=ROUND(pension,2)
firm$.emp.pension=firm$.emp.pension+pension
totpension=totpension+pension
 REM National Insurance
ni=0
FOR level=1 TO 4
  IF gross<=band(level) THEN ni=gross*ni(level):level=4
NEXT level
IF gross>band(4) THEN ni=band(4)*ni(4)
ni=ROUND(ni,2)
firm$.emp.ni=firm$.emp.ni+ni
totni=totni+ni


 REM tax based on year to date earnings
taxfree=(firm$.emp.taxcode*10)/52
taxfree=taxfree*wknum
taxable=firm$.emp.gross-firm$.emp.pension-taxfree
tax=0
IF taxable<=0 AND firm$.emp.tax=0 THEN GOTO taxend

FOR level=1 TO 5
  limit=tband(level)*wknum
  IF taxable<limit THEN tax=tax+taxable*trate(level):level=5 ELSE
  - tax=tax+limit*trate(level)
  taxable=taxable-limit
NEXT level
IF taxable>0 THEN tax=tax+taxable*trate(6)
tax=tax-firm$.emp.tax:REM deduct tax paid to date
tax=ROUND(tax,2)
firm$.emp.tax=firm$.emp.tax+tax
tottax=tottax+tax


LABEL taxend
```

```
net=gross-pension-ni-tax
firm$.emp.net=firm$.emp.net+net
totnet=totnet+net

  REM coin and note analysis
poundcash=INT(net):pencecash=(net-poundcash)*100
out$="  "
FOR pay=1 TO 3
  temp=poundcash\note(pay)
  out$=out$+STR$(temp)+"xf"+STR$(note(pay))+" "
  pounds(pay)=pounds(pay)+temp
  poundcash=poundcash MOD note(pay)
NEXT pay
out$=out$+STR$(poundcash)+"x[po]1"
pounds(4)=pounds(4)+poundcash

FOR pay=1 TO 5
  temp=pencecash\coin(pay)
  out$=out$+STR$(temp)+"x"+STR$(coin(pay))+"p "
  pennies(pay)=pennies(pay)+temp
  pencecash=pencecash MOD coin(pay)
NEXT pay
out$=out$+STR$(pencecash)+"p"
pennies(6)=pennies(6)+pencecash

  where=1:GOSUB slipout:REM screen copy
  IF streamnum<>1 THEN where=streamnum:GOSUB slipout: REM paper/disk copy
  PUT #5,firm$ AT slip

  LABEL nextslip
NEXT slip
wknum=wknum+1
IF streamnum=6 THEN CLOSE #6
GOSUB anykey

RETURN

LABEL slipout
PRINT #where,"----------------------------------------------------------------"
PRINT #where,"Ref. No. ";slip;" Name ";firm$.emp.name$
PRINT #where,"Gross Pay f";gross
PRINT #where,"Pension Cont. f";pension
PRINT #where,"National Insurance. f";ni
PRINT #where,"Tax f";tax
PRINT #where,"Net Pay f";net
PRINT #where,out$
```

185

```
PRINT #where,"-------------------------------------------------------------------"
PRINT #where
RETURN


LABEL totals
CLS
GOSUB outwhere
PRINT #streamnum,company$
PRINT #streamnum,"Number of Employees ";num
PRINT #streamnum,"Week Number ";wknum
PRINT #streamnum,"Totals to Date"
PRINT #streamnum,"Gross Pay ";totgross
PRINT #streamnum,"Pension Fund ";totpension
PRINT #streamnum,"National Insurance ";totni
PRINT #streamnum,"Income Tax ";tottax
PRINT #streamnum,"net pay ";totnet
PRINT #streamnum
PRINT #streamnum,"Coin and Note Analysis"
out$=""
FOR pay=1 TO 4
  out$=out$+STR$(pounds(pay))+"x£"+STR$(note(pay))+" "
NEXT pay
FOR pay=1 TO 6
  out$=out$+STR$(pennies(pay))+"x"+STR$(coin(pay))+"p "
NEXT pay
PRINT #streamnum,out$
GOSUB anykey
IF streamnum=6 THEN CLOSE #6
RETURN


LABEL outwhere
REPEAT
  INPUT "Output to screen, paper or disk? (S/P/D) ";a$
  a$=UPPER$(a$)
UNTIL a$="S" OR a$="P" OR a$="D"
IF a$="S" THEN streamnum=1:RETURN
IF a$="P" THEN streamnum=0:RETURN
streamnum=6
INPUT "Filename for this report ";file$
WHILE LEN(file$)<8:file$=file$+" ":WEND
file$=LEFT$(file$,8)
file$=UPPER$(file$)+".REP"
OPEN #6 OUTPUT file$
RETURN
```

```
LABEL exit
firm$.emp.name$=company$
firm$.emp.rate=num
firm$.emp.taxcode=wknum
firm$.emp.gross=totgross
firm$.emp.pension=totpension
firm$.emp.ni=totni
firm$.emp.tax=tottax
firm$.emp.net=totnet
PUT #5,firm$ AT 1
CLOSE #5
exit=1
RETURN

LABEL anykey
PRINT AT (1;21);"Press any key to go on"
WHILE i$<>"":i$=INKEY$:WEND
WHILE i$="":i$=INKEY$:WEND
RETURN
```

Chapter 14

Estate Agency System

This last program is offered as the basis for a full estate agency system, maintaining lists of properties and of clients and matching the records against each other.

As with the two earlier file-handling programs, there are Update routines for each file that will allow you to add, delete, alter or examine individual records; and the Printout facilities will list both files in full on screen, paper or disk. Additional routines will search the property file to find those that meet the requirements of an individual homeseeker; to search the clients file for potential buyers for a property; to perform a full 'Match and Mail'; and to record any sales or offers. In the 'Match and Mail' routine, the program first prints the name and address of each client, in a form that could be easily adapted for envelope labelling, then searches the property file and prints details of all properties that meet that client's specification. A flagging system ensures that properties already under offer are not included in these mailings, and that clients do not receive the same details twice.

Program structure

Initialisation

> Define records
> Open files and get master data

Main loop

> Main Loop   *menu*

Display menu
Perform option
Repeat until exit selected

Options

Update homes	*homes*
Add new	*add*
Change details	*change*
Delete from file	*remove*
View single record	*view*
Print out property file	*homerep*
Get output stream	*outwhere*
For all properties	
Print details with field headings	*showhouse*
If to disk, close stream	
Update buyers file	*buyers*
Add new	*addbuy*
Change details	*changebuy*
Delete from file	*removebuy*
View single record	*viewbuy*
Print out buyers file	*buyrep*
Get output stream	*outwhere*
For all clients	
Print details with field headings	*showbuy*
If to disk, close stream	
Search for properties for new buyer	*buysearch*
Get output stream	*outwhere*
For all properties	
Ignore if under offer	
Compare price, type and area	
If suitable, print details	*showhouse*
Mark record in buyer file as 'Mailed'	
If output to disk, close stream	
Search for buyer for new property	*homesearch*
Get output stream	*outwhere*
For all buyers	
Ignore if offer made on other property	
Compare price, type and area	
If suitable, print details	*showbuy*

Mark record in property file as 'Mailed'
If output to disk, close stream

Match and mail   *match*
   Get output stream   *outwhere*
   For all buyers
    Print name and address
    Perform search routine   *buysearch*

Record sales and offers   *sales*
   List properties under offer   *listoffers*
    Get output stream   *outwhere*
    For all properties
     If marked 'U' print details   *showhouse*

   Record an offer   *makeoffer*
    Mark property as 'U'
    Note offer price and property ref in buyer record
    Mark buyer as 'O' (Offering)

   Record sale   *sold*
    Get output stream   *outwhere*
    Print name & address of buyer
    Print name & address of vendor
    Print price and property address
    Delete property and client from file
Exit and closedown   *exit*
   Write property master data to disk
   Close property file ·
   Write buyers master data to disk
   Close buyers file

Notes

This is a long program, but a little creative editing can do much to keep the typing down to a minimum. The homes and buyers update and printout routines are all but identical. Create one set by editing the MEMBERS program, then copy and edit that to produce the second set. (The *menu*, *outwhere* and *exit* routines can also be edited in from MEMBERS.)

The search routines will need to be written from scratch, but once one has been written, the second can be created by copying and editing. Overall the amount of typing can be reduced by shortening the variable names, though this will make the program less readable and more difficult to debug or to adapt later.

In the Estate Agency System we are managing two random-access files, one for the properties — called HOMES.DAT — and one for the homeseekers — optimistically called BUYERS.DAT.

As the details needed for buyers and properties are almost identical, the same record definition is used for both files, as shown in Table 14.1.

TABLE 14.1

Field name	Property data	Buyer data
name$	Vendor's name	Buyer's name
tel$	Vendor's phone no.	Buyer's phone no.
add$	Vendor's address (3 lines)	Buyer's address
house$	Property address 2nd line = area	Alternative areas
price	Asking price	Max. price/Offer price
type$	Detached/Semi/Terrace/Flat	
beds	Number of bedrooms	
recep	Number of reception rooms	
car$	Double-/Single garage/Off-street parking/None	
gdn$	Large-/Medium-/Small-/No garden	
sold$	No/Mailed/Under offer	No/Mailed/Offering

A second definition is used for the first record in each file. In this master record almost all of the space is used to store the numbers of deleted, and therefore re-usable, records. This method of re-using the space is described in Chapter 12.

191

Estate agency program

```
REM estate agency

SCREEN #1 TEXT 80 FIXED, 22 FIXED
WINDOW #1 FULL ON

RECORD rec;name$ FIXED 30,tel$ FIXED 10,add$(1 TO 3) FIXED 20,
 - house$(1 TO 3) FIXED 20,price INTEGER,type$ FIXED 1,beds UBYTE,
 - recep UBYTE,car$ FIXED 1,gdn$ FIXED 1,sold$ FIXED 1
RECORD master;reuse$ FIXED 160,number UBYTE
all=0
blank$=STRING$(172," ")
home$=blank$
buyer$=blank$
x$=FIND$("HOMES.DAT")
OPEN #5 RANDOM "HOMES.DAT" LENGTH 172
OPEN #6 RANDOM "BUYERS.DAT" LENGTH 172
IF x$="HOMES   .DAT" THEN GOTO openold
num_homes=1
num_buyers=1
GOTO menu

LABEL openold
GET #5,check$ AT 1
spare$=check$.master.reuse$
num_homes=check$.master.number
GET #6,check$ AT 1
empty$=check$.master.reuse$
num_buyers=check$.master.number

LABEL menu
REPEAT
  CLS
  PRINT AT (25;2);"Update Homes File.............1"
  PRINT AT (25;4);"Homes Print out...............2"
  PRINT AT (25;6);"Update Buyers File............3"
  PRINT AT (25;8);"Buyers Print out..............4"
  PRINT AT (25;10);"New Buyer Search.............5"
  PRINT AT (25;12);"New Home Search..............6"
  PRINT AT (25;14);"Match and Mail...............7"
  PRINT AT (25;16);"Sales and Offers.............8"
  PRINT AT (25;18);"Exit.........................9"
```

```
  opt$=""
  WHILE opt$<"1" OR opt$>"9":opt$=INKEY$:WEND
  a=VAL(opt$)
  ON a GOSUB homes,homerep,buyers,buyrep,buysearch,homesearch,match,sales,exit
UNTIL a=9
END

LABEL homes
REPEAT
  CLS
  PRINT AT (30;3);"Update Menu"
  PRINT AT (25;6);"Add new Home...................1"
  PRINT AT (25;8);"Change Details................2"
  PRINT AT (25;10);"Remove Home from file.........3"
  PRINT AT (25;12);"View single home..............4"
  PRINT AT (25;14);"Exit..........................5"

  up$=""
  WHILE up$<"1" OR up$>"5"
    up$=INKEY$
  WEND
  up=VAL(up$)
  ON up GOSUB add,change,remove,view,out
UNTIL up=5
RETURN

LABEL add
REPEAT
  CLS
  INPUT "Vendor's name ";home$.rec.name$
  INPUT "Telephone number ";home$.rec.tel$
  INPUT "Vendor's address (Line 1)";home$.rec.add$(1)
  INPUT "Vendor's address (Line 2)";home$.rec.add$(2)
  INPUT "Vendor's address (Line 3)";home$.rec.add$(3)
  INPUT "Is the property address different (Y/N) ";a$
  IF UPPER$(a$)="Y" THEN GOTO diff
  FOR add=1 TO 3
    home$.rec.house$(add)=home$.rec.add$(add)
  NEXT add
  GOTO otherdata

  LABEL diff
  INPUT "House Address ";home$.rec.house$(1)
  INPUT "Area ";home$.rec.house$(2)
  INPUT "Town or City ";home$.rec.house$(3)
```

```
    LABEL otherdata
    INPUT "Price ";home$.rec.price
    PRINT "Type of House - Detached, Semi, Terrace, Flat."
    INPUT "(D/S/T/F)"; home$.rec.type$
    INPUT "Number of bedrooms ";home$.rec.beds
    INPUT "Number of reception rooms ";home$.rec.recep
    PRINT "Double garage, Single garage, Off-street parking, None "
    INPUT "(D/S/O/N)";home$.rec.car$
    INPUT "Garden - Large,Medium,Small,None (L/M/S/N)";home$.rec.gdn$
    home$.rec.sold$="N"
    IF LEN(spare$)>0 THEN homenum=ASC(LEFT$(spare$,1)):spare$=MID$(spare$,2)
     - ELSE num_homes=num_homes+1:homenum=num_homes
    PUT #5,home$ AT homenum
    PRINT "Property Reference Number is ";homenum
    INPUT "Another new property? (Y/N) ";again$
UNTIL UPPER$(again$)="N"
RETURN


LABEL change
REPEAT
  GOSUB gethome
  IF homenum=0 THEN GOTO changed
  GOSUB shortshow
  PRINT "Current Price ";home$.rec.price
  INPUT "Change Price (Y/N) ";a$
  IF UPPER$(a$)="Y" THEN INPUT "New Price ";home$.rec.price
  PUT #5,home$ AT homenum
  LABEL changed
  INPUT "Another property (Y/N) ";again$
UNTIL UPPER$(again$)="N"
RETURN


LABEL remove
REPEAT
  GOSUB gethome
  IF homenum=0 THEN GOTO removed
  GOSUB shortshow
  INPUT "Check. Really delete this? (Y/N) ";a$
  IF UPPER$(a$)="N" THEN GOTO removed
  PUT #5,blank$ AT homenum
  spare$=spare$+CHR$(homenum)

  LABEL removed
  INPUT "Another property (Y/N) ";again$
UNTIL UPPER$(again$)="N"
RETURN
```

```
LABEL shortshow
PRINT "Reference Number ";homenum
PRINT "Vendor ";home$.rec.name$
PRINT "Address :"
FOR add=1 TO 3
  PRINT home$.rec.house$(add)
NEXT add
RETURN

LABEL view
GOSUB outwhere
REPEAT
  GOSUB gethome
  IF homenum>0 THEN GOSUB showhouse
  INPUT "Another property (Y/N) ";again$
UNTIL UPPER$(again$)="N"
RETURN

LABEL showhouse
IF home$=blank$ THEN RETURN
PRINT #where,"Reference number: ";homenum
PRINT #where,"Vendor: ";home$.rec.name$
PRINT #where,"Vendor's address "
FOR add=1 TO 3
  PRINT #where,home$.rec.add$(add)
NEXT add
PRINT #where,"Tel: ";home$.rec.tel$
PRINT #where,"The Property"
FOR add=1 TO 3
  PRINT #where,home$.rec.house$(add)
NEXT add
PRINT #where,"Price ";home$.rec.price
PRINT #where,"Detached, Semi, Terrace, Flat.";home$.rec.type$
PRINT #where,"No.bedrooms ";home$.rec.beds
PRINT #where,"No.reception ";home$.rec.recep
PRINT #where,"Double/Single garage, Off-street, None ";home$.rec.car$
PRINT #where,"Garden - Large, Medium, Small, None ";home$.rec.gdn$
PRINT #where,"Status - New, Mailed, Under offer ";home$.rec.sold$
RETURN

LABEL gethome
CLS
INPUT "Property Reference Number (0 if not known )";homenum
IF homenum>0 THEN GET #5,home$ AT homenum:GOTO getout
num=0
INPUT "Address (Line 1) ";add$
```

```
WHILE homenum=0 AND NOT(EOF(#5))
  num=num+1
  GET #5,home$ AT num
  IF UPPER$(home$.rec.house$(1))=UPPER$(add$) THEN homenum=num
WEND

LABEL getout
IF homenum>0 THEN PRINT "Property Address ";home$.rec.house$(1)
IF homenum=0 THEN PRINT "Property not found"
GOSUB anykey
RETURN

LABEL homerep
GOSUB outwhere
PRINT #where,"PROPERTY FILE"
PRINT #where
FOR homenum=2 TO num_homes
  GET #5,home$ AT homenum
  GOSUB showhouse
  PRINT #where
NEXT homenum
IF where=7 THEN CLOSE #7
IF where=1 THEN GOSUB anykey
RETURN

LABEL buyers
REPEAT
  CLS
  PRINT AT (30;3);"Buyers Update Menu"
  PRINT AT (25;6);"Add new Buyer.................1"
  PRINT AT (25;8);"Change Details................2"
  PRINT AT (25;10);"Remove Buyer from File........3"
  PRINT AT (25;12);"View single Buyer.............4"
  PRINT AT (25;14);"Exit..........................5"

  up$=""
  WHILE up$<"1" OR up$>"5":up$=INKEY$:WEND
  up=VAL(up$)
  ON up GOSUB addbuy,changebuy,removebuy,viewbuy,out
UNTIL up=5
RETURN

LABEL addbuy
REPEAT
  CLS
  INPUT "Buyer's name ";buyer$.rec.name$
```

```
    INPUT "Buyer's address (Line 1)";buyer$.rec.add$(1)
    INPUT "Buyer's address (Line 2)";buyer$.rec.add$(2)
    INPUT "Buyer's address (Line 3)";buyer$.rec.add$(3)
    INPUT "Telephone number ";buyer$.rec.tel$
    PRINT "Requirements"
    INPUT "Preferred Area ";buyer$.rec.house$(1)
    INPUT "Alternative Area 1 ";buyer$.rec.house$(2)
    INPUT "Alternative Area 2 ";buyer$.rec.house$(3)
    INPUT "Maximum Price ";buyer$.rec.price
    PRINT "Type of House - Detached, Semi, Terrace, Flat."
    INPUT "(D/S/T/F)",buyer$.rec.type$
    INPUT "Number of bedrooms ";buyer$.rec.beds
    INPUT "Number of reception rooms ";buyer$.rec.recep
    PRINT "Double garage, Single garage, Off-street parking, None "
    INPUT "(D/S/O/N)";buyer$.rec.car$
    INPUT "Garden - Large,Medium,Small,None (L/M/S/N)";buyer$.rec.gdn$
    buyer$.rec.sold$="N"
    IF LEN(empty$)>0 THEN buynum=ASC(LEFT$(empty$,1)):empty$=MID$(empty$,2)
      - ELSE num_buyers=num_buyers+1:buynum=num_buyers
    PUT #6,buyer$ AT buynum
    PRINT "Buyer Reference Number is ";buynum
    INPUT "Another new client? (Y/N) ";again$
  UNTIL UPPER$(again$)="N"
  RETURN


  LABEL changebuy
  REPEAT
    GOSUB getbuy
    IF buynum=0 THEN GOTO changedb
    PRINT "Reference Number ";buynum
    PRINT "Buyer: ";buyer$.rec.name$
    PRINT "Current Maximum ";buyer$.rec.price
    INPUT "Change Price (Y/N) ";a$
    IF UPPER$(a$)="Y" THEN INPUT "New Price ";buyer$.rec.price
    PRINT "Current Status ";buyer$.rec.sold$
    temp$=buyer$.rec.sold$
    INPUT "Change Status (Y/N) ";a$
    IF UPPER$(a$)="Y" THEN INPUT "Mailed, Under Offer (M/U) ";temp$
    buyer$.rec.sold$=UPPER$(temp$)
    PUT #6,buyer$ AT buynum

    LABEL changedb
    INPUT "Another property (Y/N) ";again$
  UNTIL UPPER$(again$)="N"
  RETURN
```

```
LABEL removebuy
REPEAT
  GOSUB getbuy
  IF buynum=0 THEN GOTO removedb
  PRINT "Reference Number ";buynum
  PRINT "Buyer: ";buyer$.rec.name$
  INPUT "Check. Really delete this? (Y/N) ";a$
  IF UPPER$(a$)="N" THEN GOTO removed
  PUT #6,blank$ AT buynum
  empty$=empty$+CHR$(buynum)

  LABEL removedb
  INPUT "Another buyer (Y/N) ";again$
UNTIL UPPER$(again$)="N"
RETURN

LABEL viewbuy
GOSUB outwhere
REPEAT
  GOSUB getbuy
  IF buynum>0 THEN GOSUB showbuy
  INPUT "Another buyer (Y/N) ";again$
UNTIL UPPER$(again$)="N"
RETURN

LABEL showbuy
IF buyer$=blank$ THEN RETURN
PRINT #where,"Reference Number: ";buynum
PRINT #where,"Buyer: ";buyer$.rec.name$
PRINT #where,"Tel:   ";buyer$.rec.tel$
PRINT #where,"Address ";buyer$.rec.add$(1)
PRINT #where,"        ";buyer$.rec.add$(2)
PRINT #where,"        ";buyer$.rec.add$(3)
PRINT #where,"Areas "
FOR add=1 TO 3
PRINT #where,"        ";buyer$.rec.house$(add)
NEXT add
PRINT #where,"Maximum Price ";buyer$.rec.price
PRINT #where,"Detached, Semi, Terrace, Flat.";buyer$.rec.type$
PRINT #where,"No.bedrooms ";buyer$.rec.beds
PRINT #where,"No.reception ";buyer$.rec.recep
PRINT #where,"Double/Single garage, Off-street, None ";buyer$.rec.car$
PRINT #where,"Garden - Large, Medium, Small, None ";buyer$.rec.gdn$
PRINT #where,"Status - New, Mailed, Offering ";buyer$.rec.sold$
RETURN
```

```
LABEL getbuy
CLS
INPUT "Buyer's Reference Number (0 if not known )";buynum
IF buynum>0 THEN GET #6,buyer$ AT buynum:GOTO gotbuy
num=0
INPUT "Buyer's Name ";name$
WHILE buynum=0 AND NOT(EOF(#6))
  num=num+1
  GET #6,buyer$ AT num
  IF UPPER$(buyer$.rec.name$)=UPPER$(name$) THEN buynum=num
WEND

LABEL gotbuy
IF buynum>0 THEN PRINT "Buyers name ";buyer$.rec.name$
IF buynum=0 THEN PRINT "Buyer not found"
GOSUB anykey
RETURN

LABEL buyrep
GOSUB outwhere
PRINT #where,"BUYERS FILE"
PRINT #where
FOR buynum=2 TO num_buyers
  GET #6,buyer$ AT buynum
  GOSUB showbuy
  PRINT #where
NEXT buynum
IF where=7 THEN CLOSE #7
IF where=1 THEN GOSUB anykey
RETURN

LABEL out
REM dummy paragraph to cope with on..gosub ..
RETURN

LABEL outwhere
CLS
INPUT "Output to Screen, Paper or Disk? (S/P/D) ";a$
IF UPPER$(a$)="S" THEN where=1:RETURN
IF UPPER$(a$)="P" THEN where=0:RETURN
where=7
INPUT "Filename for this report";file$
file$=UPPER$(LEFT$(file$,8))+".REP"
OPEN #7 OUTPUT file$
RETURN
```

```
LABEL buysearch
IF all=1 THEN GOTO searchpara
message$="Search for homes for new buyer":GOSUB outwhere
GOSUB getbuy
IF buynum=0 THEN RETURN
LABEL searchpara
price=buyer$.rec.price
type$=buyer$.rec.type$
area$=""
FOR add=1 TO 3
  area$=area$+UPPER$(buyer$.rec.house$(add))
NEXT add
found=0
FOR homenum=2 TO num_homes
  GET #5,home$ AT homenum
  IF UPPER$(home$.rec.sold$)="U" THEN GOTO searchend
  IF home$.rec.price>price THEN GOTO searchend
  IF home$.rec.type$<>type$ THEN GOTO searchend
  IF INSTR(area$,UPPER$(home$.rec.house$(2)))=0 THEN GOTO searchend
   REM checks only price, type and area
  found=found+1
  GOSUB showhouse
  IF all=1 THEN home$.rec.sold$="M":PUT #5,home$ AT homenum

  LABEL searchend
NEXT homenum
PRINT #where,"Possible Homes Found: ";found
buyer$.rec.sold$="M"
 REM mark as Mailed
PUT #6,buyer$ AT buynum
IF all=1 THEN RETURN
IF where=7 THEN CLOSE #7
IF where=1 THEN GOSUB anykey
RETURN

LABEL homesearch
message$="Search for possible buyers":GOSUB outwhere
GOSUB gethome
IF homenum=0 THEN RETURN
price=home$.rec.price
type$=home$.rec.type$
found=0
FOR buynum=2 TO num_buyers
  GET #6,buyer$ AT buynum
  IF UPPER$(buyer$.rec.sold$)="O" THEN GOTO nextsearch
  IF buyer$.rec.price<price THEN GOTO nextsearch
```

```
    IF buyer$.rec.type$<>type$ THEN GOTO nextsearch
    area$=""
    FOR add=1 TO 3
      area$=area$+UPPER$(buyer$.rec.house$(add))
    NEXT add
    IF INSTR(area$,UPPER$(home$.rec.house$(2)))=0 THEN GOTO nextsearch
     REM checks only price, type and area
    found=found+1
    GOSUB showbuy

    LABEL nextsearch
NEXT buynum
home$.rec.sold$="M"
 REM mark as Mailed
PUT #5,home$ AT homenum
PRINT #where,"Possible Buyers Found: ";found
IF where=7 THEN CLOSE #7
IF where=1 THEN GOSUB anykey
RETURN


LABEL match
all=1
message$="Full Match and Mail Routine":GOSUB outwhere
FOR buynum=2 TO num_buyers
  GET #6,buyer$ AT buynum
  PRINT #where,buyer$.rec.name$
  FOR n=1 TO 3
    PRINT #where,buyer$.rec.add$(n)
  NEXT n
  PRINT #where
  GOSUB buysearch
NEXT buynum
IF where=7 THEN CLOSE #7
IF where=1 THEN GOSUB anykey
all=0
RETURN


LABEL sales
REPEAT
  CLS
  PRINT AT (25;4);"List properties under offer..........1"
  PRINT AT (25;6);"Record Offer made....................2"
  PRINT AT (25;8);"Record Sale..........................3"
  PRINT AT (25;10);"Return to Main Menu.................4"
  ky$=INKEY$
  WHILE ky$<"1" OR ky$>"4"
```

```
    ky$=INKEY$
  WEND


  IF ky$="1" THEN GOSUB listoffers
  IF ky$="2" THEN GOSUB makeoffer
  IF ky$="3" THEN GOSUB sold

UNTIL ky$="4"
RETURN


LABEL listoffers
message$="List of Properties under Offer":GOSUB outwhere
FOR homenum=2 TO num_homes
  GET #5,home$ AT homenum
  IF home$.rec.sold$="U" THEN GOSUB showhouse
NEXT homenum
IF where=7 THEN CLOSE #7
IF where=1 THEN GOSUB anykey
RETURN


LABEL makeoffer
REPEAT
  GOSUB geth^me
  IF homenum=0 THEN RETURN
  home$.rec.sold$="U":PUT #5,home$ AT homenum
  GOSUB getbuy
  IF buynum=0 THEN RETURN
  FOR add=1 TO 3
    buyer$.rec.house$(add)=home$.rec.house$(add)
  NEXT add
  INPUT "Offered Price ";price
  buyer$.rec.price=price
  buyer$.rec.beds=homenum
  buyer$.rec.sold$="O":PUT #6,buyer$ AT buynum
  INPUT "Another Offer? (Y/N) ";a$
UNTIL UPPER$(a$)="N"
RETURN


LABEL sold
message$="Recording Sale":GOSUB outwhere
GOSUB getbuy
homenum=buyer$.rec.beds
GET #5,home$ AT homenum
PRINT #where,"Buyer ";buyer$.rec.name$
FOR n=1 TO 3
  PRINT #where,buyer$.rec.add$(n)
```

```
NEXT n
PRINT #where
PRINT #where,"Vendor ";home$.rec.name$
FOR n=1 TO 3
  PRINT #where,home$.rec.add$(n)
NEXT n
PRINT #where,"Price ";buyer$.rec.price
PRINT #where,"Property "
FOR add=1 TO 3
  PRINT #where,home$.rec.house$(add)
NEXT add
PUT #6,blank$ AT buynum
empty$=empty$+CHR$(buynum)
PUT #5,blank$ AT homenum
spare$=spare$+CHR$(homenum)
IF where=7 THEN CLOSE #7
IF where=1 THEN GOSUB anykey
RETURN

LABEL anykey
PRINT
PRINT "Press any key to continue"
ky$=""
WHILE ky$="":ky$=INKEY$:WEND
RETURN

LABEL exit
home$.master.reuse$=spare$
home$.master.number=num_homes
PUT #5,home$ AT 1
buyer$.master.reuse$=empty$
buyer$.master.number=num_buyers
PUT #6,buyer$ AT 1
CLOSE #5
CLOSE #6
RETURN
```

BASIC2 COMMANDS AND FUNCTIONS

General rules

All **graphics** and **text** commands may include the window or stream number, immediately after the keyword, e.g. **BOX #2, 20;50,200,150.** If omitted, the command will draw in the current window, or write to the current stream.

File-handling commands must include the stream number, as this is essential for identifying the file.

Where a command can take **options**, these may be written in any order after the main part of the command, and should be separated by spaces.

If a command or function requires a **number**, this can be a literal number, a variable, or any expression yielding a numeric value.

Where a **string** is wanted, this may be a literal string, a variable, or a function that produces a string value.

Alphabetical summary of commands

ADDKEY #stream KEY number INDEX number adds a new sorting KEY for the current record in a file. If the INDEX number is omitted, the current index is assumed.

ADDREC #stream,string KEY number INDEX number used instead of **PUT** to add a record to a keyed file.

BOX x;y,width,height options draws a box, with x;y as the bottom left corner. These standard GRAPHICs **options** are available: COLOUR, FILL, MODE, STYLE and WIDTH; plus the special **ROUNDED**, which rounds off the corners. See GRAPHICS.

CHDIR name changes directory. Note that if the command includes a drive letter, this must be given as a capital letter. This is the form to be used within a program. If operating in the Dialogue window, use **CD name** instead.

CIRCLE x;y,radius options draws a circle as specified. The standard **options** are available, plus:
   PART start,end draws an arc between the angles given.
   START number END number selects end-styles for the line.
See GRAPHICS.

CLEAR erases the working memory, including all arrays and other variables, loop controls and GOSUB return points. File streams are closed.

CLEAR RESET performs a CLEAR and restores all streams, screens and windows to their default state. To be recommended when experiments with windows have gone astray!

CLOSE #stream closes the file linked to the stream number, ensuring that an data in the buffer is written to disk first.

CLOSE WINDOW number closes the given window.

CLS #stream clears the screen identified by the stream number.

CONSOLIDATE number brings a keyed file and its index file up to date after records have been changed.

CONT or **F7** continues a program after a CTRL-C break, or STOP.

DATA value,value . . . marks the start of a line of data that will be READ into variables. Quotes are not needed around strings unless they contain spaces or commas.

DEF FNname(variable(s))=expression defines a new function for use later in the program, e.g. **DEF FNcube(n) = n*n*n**. After this command has been executed, the statement **answer=FNcube(3)**, for example, would assign the value 27 to **answer**.

DELKEY #stream KEY number deletes the key for the current record − if there is only one key, then the record will also be deleted.

DIM var(dimensions) type defines and initialises an array. An array may have any number of **dimensions**, and the range of subscript values may be set, e.g. **DIM years(49 TO 87)**. The **type** definition is used only where a specific type of numeric variable is to be used. You cannot redefine an existing array without first erasing it with CLEAR.

DISPLAY filename prints the contents of a file on screen. The Dialogue equivalent is TYPE.

DRIVE letter selects a drive − this must be a single letter in quotes and in capitals.

EDIT switches from Dialogue to Edit window.

ELLIPSE x;y,radius,aspect options is identical to the **CIRCLE** command except for the inclusion of the **aspect** value which determines the horizontal to vertical ratio.

ELLIPTICAL PIE x;y,radius,aspect,start,end is identical to **PIE** with the addition of the **aspect** ratio.

END marks the end of a program. A well-structured program will only have one END, but it is possible to have any number of ENDs.

ERROR number simulates the given error. Useful for testing error-trapping routines.

FILES file-spec is used within a program to show the files in a directory. The file-specification is optional, but if given will restrict the search to those filenames that match the specifications. Use DIR in the Dialogue window.

FLOOD x;y,boundary__colour options starts from x;y and fills the area up to the limits set by the boundary colour. If not specified, the fill will stop at the nearest lines. If the area is not completely enclosed by lines, then the flood will escape! Options are COLOUR, MODE and FILL. (Not present in some versions of GEM.)

FOR var=start TO end STEP size . . . NEXT var repeats the set of commands between the **FOR** and **NEXT** lines. The value of **var** is altered by **size** each time the **NEXT** line is reached, until it is equal to or greater than **end**. If omitted, the **STEP** size is taken to be +1.

FORWARD distance options (or FD) − a turtle graphics command that draws a line in the current turtle direction. All normal drawing options are available. Include **MOVE** at the start to move the turtle without drawing.

GET #stream, string transfers a record from a random file into the named string.

GOSUB label-name causes the program to jump to the named subroutine and to return to the jump-point afterwards.

GOTO label-name causes the program to jump to the named routine.

GRAPHICS #stream, options sets the default values for the given options:
  CURSOR style number.
  COLOUR number selects foreground ink colour.
  FILL ONLY WITH number selects pattern for filling. If ONLY is omitted, the
    outline will be drawn.
  MARKER SIZE value sets the size of the marker for plotting.
  MARKER style-number.
  MODE number selects: 1 overwrite, 2 transparent (foreground colour only),
    3 XOR and 4 reverse transparent (background only, but shown in foreground
    colour).
  ROUNDED − BOX corners rounded, not square.
  STYLE number selects style for outline.
  WIDTH number selects width of line for outlining.

IF condition(s) THEN command(s)1 ELSE command(s)2 If the conditions are met, then the command, or set of commands, in the next part of the line are executed. If they are not met, then those commands following **ELSE** will be executed. This second part of the line may be omitted; in which case the program will do nothing if the conditions are not met.

INPUT #stream, AT(col;row); prompt;variable(s) gets data from the keyboard, echoing the input on the selected **stream**. The **prompt** must be a literal string.

KEYSPEC #stream, INDEX number variable__type UNIQUE on/off defines an index for a keyed file. The UNIQUE switch is optional, and left ON by default.

KILL filename deletes a file from within a program. In the Dialogue window, use DEL or ERASE instead.

LABEL name marks a line in the program for use with **GOSUB** or **GOTO** jumps.

LEFT angle (or LT) turns the turtle through an angle anti-clockwise.

LET variable=value assigns a value. **LET** is optional, and would normally only be included to improve the readability of a program.

LINE x;y,x1;y1,... options draws a continuous line, linking together the points in the list. There is no limit to the number of points, except that imposed by the length of a Basic line. The standard Graphics options apply.

LINE INPUT AT(col;row); prompt;variable(s) is similar to the simple INPUT, but this can only be used for strings. Leading spaces are taken into the string, as are commas, which would normally mark the end of the variable.

LOCATE col;row moves the cursor to a given position on a text screen. As the PRINT AT and INPUT AT option will perform the same task, this command is of limited value.

LPRINT equivalent to **PRINT #0** − outputs to printer.

LSET var$=string assigns a value to an existing string, without changing the length of **var$**. The new string data will be justified to the left, and truncated or padded with spaces to the right as necessary.

MKDIR name creates a new directory from within a program. Use MD within the Dialogue window.

MOVE x;y relocates the cursor on the graphics screen.

NAME old-file AS new-file renames a file from within a program. The Dialogue equivalent is **REN old-file new-file**.

NEW erases the current program and its variables from memory.

ON ERROR GOTO label-name redirects the program to the named routine where your error-handling will be performed.

ON ERROR GOTO 0 cancels this error-trapping. Thereafter, any errors will be reported on screen as normal.

ON var GOSUB label__1,label__2,...label__n
ON var GOTO label__1,label__2,...label__n − The value of **var** must be between 1 and the number of label names in the list. The program will jump to that routine whose position in the list corresponds to the value of **var**, e.g. **ON opt GOSUB add,show,leave,listall,parun,totals,exit**. If **choice** has the value 4, then the program will jump to the **listall** routine.

OPEN #stream INPUT filename opens a sequential file for reading.

OPEN #stream OLD APPEND filename opens a sequential file so that data can be added to the end of it. OLD is optional, and will give an error report if no file of that name exists already.

OPEN #stream NEW OUTPUT filename opens a sequential file for writing. The optional NEW will give an error report if there is already a file of that name.

OPEN #stream RANDOM filename INDEX index-file LENGTH number__bytes opens a random access file for reading and writing. INDEX is only required for KEYed files. LENGTH will be 128 characters unless specified.

OPEN #stream DEVICE number enables output to a graphics device.

OPEN #stream PRINT number enables output to a specific printer.

OPEN #stream WINDOW number opens a window − the default settings link WINDOWs 1 and 2 with STREAMS 1 and 2.

OPTION type where **type** can be:
  DEGREES or **RADIANS** − selects angle mode;
  CURRENCY$/DATE/DECIMAL − sets PRINT formats;
  TRAP ON/OFF determines how the system deals with undefined variables.

OPTION RUN protects a Basic2 program, or routine, by disabling Break.

OPTION STOP re-enables Break.

PIE x;y,radius, start,end options draws a segment of a circle between the given start and end angles where 0 is at 3 o'clock and the angles are measured anti-clockwise. Normal graphics options apply.

PLOT x;y,x1;y1.... options plots markers at a set of points.

POINT bearing turns the turtle to point in a given direction.

PRINT #stream, item(s) where the **items** can be variables, literal strings and numbers or any combination of the following, separated either by semi-colons, commas or spaces:
  AT (col;row); **TAB (col)**; **ZONE (width)** − position;
  COLOUR (num) or **COLOR (num)** − colour;
  EFFECTS (bit-pattern); **MODE (num)** − appearance;
  POINTS (size); **ADJUST (size)**; **FONT (num)** − font size and type;
  ANGLE (value) − normally rounded to multiples of 90 degrees.

PUT #stream, string writes a record in a random-access file.

QUIT or **SYSTEM** exits Basic2.

RANDOMIZE number sets the seed for the pseudo-random number generator. If number is omitted, the current value of **TIME** is used. For any given **number** the subsequent series of random numbers will always be the same.

READ var,var1,var2... assigns values from a **DATA** line, starting at the current data-pointer position, to a variable, or series of variables. As each item is READ, the data pointer is moved on to the next.

RECORD name;field__1 type,field__2 type... defines a record structure as a set of field names. If the field **type** is omitted, a real number type is assumed.

REM prefaces a remark. Any Basic commands further along the line will be ignored. The **REM** statement may be at end of a multi-statement line, except for those that start with **DATA**.

REPEAT...UNTIL condition The commands within this loop will be repeated until the condition is met. Even where the condition is true before the start of the loop, the commands will be performed once. Contrast this with the **WHILE...WEND** loop.

RESET drive-letter resets the drive when a disk is changed.

RESTORE label-name moves the data-pointer to the first **DATA** line after the named point. If **label-name** is omitted, the data-pointer is moved to the first **DATA** line in the program.

RESUME label-name will re-start the program at the named point after an error. If **label-name** is omitted, the program will return to the point at which the error occurred.

RESUME NEXT restarts the program at the command after that which caused the error.

RETURN jumps back from a subroutine to the command after **GOSUB**.

RIGHT angle (or RT) turns the graphics turtle to the right.

RMDIR directory erases a directory from within a program. Use RD instead in the Dialogue window.

RSET var$=string as **LSET** assigns a value to an existing variable without changing the length of that variable. The new data will be justified to the right, and truncated or padded with spaces at the left.

RUN starts a program at the beginning and erases all variables.

RUN label-name starts the program at a named point. To restart a program, retaining the previous values of variables (very useful while testing), use **GOTO label-name**.

SCREEN #stream type width FIXED, height FIXED options where **type** may be **GRAPHICS** or **TEXT**; **width** and **height** may be omitted (in which case the current size will prevail) and, if given, need not be **FIXED**. Additionally, **TEXT** screens may be defined as **FLEXIBLE**, giving them a size of 2000 characters, of which as much as possible will be displayed in the linked window. The **options** are:

    MAXIMUM width,height beyond which the linked window may not be stretched;
    MINIMUM width,height similarly limiting the window size;
    UNIT width,height setting the increments in which the window size may be changed;
    INFORMATION ON/OFF controlling the presence of an information line beneath the TITLE line.

SET options selects the default values for the PRINT options. See **PRINT**.

SHAPE x;y,x1;y1,x2;y2,.... draws a shape by joining the co-ordinates with lines.

STOP halts program execution. The command is normally used as a temporary measure, to set break-points in a program while testing.

STREAM #number selects the current stream. Subsequently, the **#stream** parameter may be omitted from an graphic or text commands or functions accessing this stream.

SWAP var__1,var__2 exchanges the contents of two variables.

TEXT control − management command for TEXT screens. The **control** option may be any one of **CLEAR EOL/BOL/EOS/BOS**. Wipes from the cursor on to the end, or back to the beginning of the line or of the screen:

    CLEAR LINE/SCREEN wipes a whole line or screen;
    DELETE erases a character and pulls the text back one space;
    DELETE LINE erases a line and moves the text up;
    INSERT LINE moves the text down one line;
    FEED number moves the cursor down a number of lines.

USER ORIGIN x;y moves the origin (point 0;0) on the graphics screen to a new position, as defined by the user co-ordinates.

USER SPACE width,height defines a new user co-ordinate system. If **height** is omitted, Basic2 will calculate a suitable value to keep the aspect ratio constant.

WHILE condition .... WEND offers an alternative to **REPEAT...UNTIL** for looping through a set of lines. Note that with this structure, the commands within the loop are never performed if the condition is met at the start of the routine.

WINDOW CLOSE removes a window from the visible screen.

WINDOW CURSOR ON/OFF controls the cursor display.

WINDOW FULL ON/OFF switches window between full screen and previously defined size.

WINDOW INFORMATION string defines text for the information line.

WINDOW MOUSE number selects the mouse pointer style.

WINDOW OPEN brings a window into view.

WINDOW PLACE x;y positions a window. Note that the x;y specifies the bottom left corner and that **pixels** are used, not the user co-ordinate system.

WINDOW SCROLL x;y moves the virtual screen beneath the window to the point x;y, but note that, as this is a virtual, not the actual screen, **user co-ordinates** are used, not pixels.

WINDOW SIZE width,height sets the size of the window − in **pixels**.

WINDOW TITLE string defines the title for the window.

ZONE width sets the width of the print zone (used with comma separators) in the Dialogue window.

Alphabetical summary of functions

ABS(number) lops the negative sign, if present. Use it to find the absolute difference between two numbers. Thus, **ABS(10−4) = ABS(4−10) = 6**.

ACOS(number) converts a cosine value back into an angle − this will be in radians, unless the OPTION DEGREES command has been used.

AND − logical operator. In a line such as **IF condition_1 AND condition_2 THEN ...**, both conditions must be met for the next command to be performed.

ASC(character) returns the ASCII number of the character.

ASIN(number) converts a sine value into the related angle.

ATAN(number) (or ATN) converts a tangent value into an angle.

ATAN2(x,y) gives the bearing of the point x;y from the origin.

BIN$(number,size) converts a numerical value to a binary string, e.g. **a$=BIN$(42,8)** assigns **"0011010"** to a$.

BUTTON (number), where 1 means the left button of the mouse, and 2 the right. The value returned will be − 1 if the button is not pressed at the time of testing.

CEILING (number) rounds a value up to the nearest integer.

CHDIR$ drive gives the current directory.

CHR$(number) gives the character relating to that ASCII value.

CINT(number) rounds a number to a 32-bit integer.

COS(angle) gives the cosine of an angle.

CURRENCY$ gives the string in use for currency signs.

DATE date-string, where **date-string** is a date in standard format, converts the string to the number of days since 31/12/1899. If **date-string** is omitted, today's date is assumed.

DATE$(days) is the inverse of **DATE$**. If **days** is omitted, today's date will be returned.

DEG(angle) converts an angle from radians to degrees.

DIMENSIONS (name()) gives the number of dimensions in the named array.

DISTANCE(x;y) gives the distance in user co-ordinates from the current cursor position to the point.

EOF(#stream) tests for the end of the file and returns a TRUE/FALSE value.

ERR returns the number of the error which has occurred. **PRINT ERR** will display it on screen. **problem=ERR** will transfer it to the variable **problem** for treatment within the program.

ERROR$(number) will convert the error number to an error message.

EXP(number) raises *e* to the power of **number**.

EXTENT print_options string returns the horizontal space, in user co-ordinates, that the string would need if printed.

FIND$(file-spec,n) looks for a file matching the specification, starting at the **n**th in the directory. If found, the full filename is returned.

FINDDIR$(dir-spec,n), as **FIND$**, but for directories.

FIX(number) (or TRUNC) lops off the decimal fraction to leave an integer.

FLOOR(number) (or INT) the opposite of **CEILING**, this rounds numbers to the nearest lower integer.

FRAC(number) − the opposite of **FIX** − this lops off the integer, leaving the decimal fraction.

FRE gives the number of bytes of free space in memory.

HEADING gives the current direction of the turtle.

HEX$(number,size) converts a number to a hexadecimal string, e.g. **a$=HEX$(42,4)** assigns "002A" to a$.

INKEY gives the number of the key that is pressed. If no key is down at the time, −1 is returned. Survey the keyboard with this routine (press ESC to exit):
```
REPEAT
   ky=INKEY
   IF ky>-1 THEN PRINT ky
UNTIL ky=27
```

INKEY$ gives the ASCII character of a key press. While almost all keys return values through **INKEY**, no matter what the status of the CTRL, ALT and SHIFT keys, only printing characters are shown up by **INKEY$**.

INPUT$(number) accepts **number** of characters from the keyboard, without displaying them on screen. Useful for passwords.

INSTR(n,main__string,possible__match) checks through the **main__string**, from the **n**th character (or the start if not given), to find a sub-string that matches the second string. If found, it returns the position of the first matching letter.

KEY(#stream) or **KEY$(#stream)** gives the data in the key field of the current record of a keyed file.

LEFT$(string,number) takes the given number of characters from the left of a string. Equivalent to **string(TO number)**.

LEN(string) gives the number of characters in a string.

LOC(#stream) returns the position number of the current record in a random file.

LOF(#stream) gives the length of a file in bytes.

LOG(number) converts a number to a natural logarithm to base e.

LOG10(number) converts a number to a logarithm to base 10.

LOWER(array(),dimension__number) gives the lowest subscript value for a dimension of an array. The number is not needed for one-dimensional arrays.

LOWER$(string) converts a string to lower case.

MAX(num__1,num__2,num__3,..) picks out the highest value from a set of numeric values.

MID$(string,start,number) where the function appears on the right-hand side of an assignment, it slices a substring from within a string. If **number** is omitted, then the slice will include all the characters to the end of the string. It may also be used for assignment, **MID$(string,start,num)=a$**. Here, the whole of the assigned string will be taken in if **num** is omitted. The same function could be performed by **string(start TO end)**.

MIN(n__1,n__2,n__3,...) − opposite of **MAX**.

MOD − arithmetic operator. This gives the remainder in integer division. **23 MOD 5=3**. The reverse slash \ tells you the number of times the divisor will go into the dividend. **23\5 = 4**.

NOT expression − logical operator. This reverses the truth of a logical expression.

OR − logical operator. In a line such as **IF condition__1 OR condition__2 THEN** ..., if either or both of the conditions are true, the next command will be performed.

OSERR gives the code number of an error at operating system level.

PI returns the mathematical constant.

POINTSIZE(font__number,points) converts a point-size specification to the nearest (smaller) available point-size for that font.

POS gives the current column number of the text cursor.

POSITION$(#stream) gives the position of the current record of a file, in string form.

RAD(angle) − opposite of **DEG**. This converts angles from degrees to radians.

RIGHT$(string,number) takes the given number of characters from the right of a string. Equivalent to **string(number TO)**

RND(number) produces a random integer in the range 1 to **number**. If **number** is omitted, the random will be a decimal fraction in the range 0 to 1.

ROUND(number,places) rounds a number. Where **places** is positive, it determines the number of decimal places; if negative, the number is rounded to **places** powers of ten. For example, **ROUND(1234.5678,2) = 1234.56**, but **ROUND(1234.5678,−2) = 1200**.

SGN(number) gives the sign (positive or negative), in the form −1, 0 or 1.

SIN(angle) gives the sine of an angle.

SQR(number) gives the square root of a number.

STR$(number) converts a number into string form.

STRING$(number,char) copies the single character,**char**, given as a literal or as an ASCII code, into a string of **number** length.

TAN(angle) gives the tangent of an angle.

TIME − divide this value by 100 to get the number of seconds since midnight, as measured on the internal clock.

TOWARD(x;y) − similar to **ATAN2** − this gives the bearing of a point from the turtle.

UPPER(array(),dimension__number) − opposite of **LOWER...**

UPPER$(string) converts a string to upper-case characters.

VAL(string) gives the numeric value, if any, of a string.

VPOS gives the current line number of the text cursor.

WHOLE$(string) assigns the whole of a fixed-length string, padding out with spaces if necessary. Nul characters in fixed-length strings would normally be ignored in assignments.

XACTUAL − width of a window in pixels.

XBAR − width of the right bar in pixels.

XCELL − width of a character cell in user co-ordinates.

XDEVICE − width of a device in pixels.

XMETRES − width of the output device in metres.

XMOUSE − x co-ordinate of the mouse cursor, in pixels.

XOR − logical operator. In a line such as **IF condition__1 XOR condition__2 THEN ...**, one of the conditions, but not both, must be true if the next command is to be performed.

XPIXEL − width of a pixel in user co-ordinates.

XPLACE − x co-ordinate of the bottom left of a window on the visible screen, in pixels.

XPOS − x co-ordinate of the cursor in user co-ordinates.

XSCROLL − x co-ordinate of the bottom left of the window in the virtual screen, in user co-ordinates.

XUSABLE − width of the available screen, in pixels.

XVIRTUAL − width of the screen in user co-ordinates.

XWINDOW − width of a window in pixels.

YACTUAL − height of a window in pixels.

YASPECT − aspect ratio of the user co-ordinates.

YBAR − height of the bottom bar in pixels.

YCELL − height of a character cell in user co-ordinates.

YDEVICE − height of a device in pixels.

YMETRES − height of the output device in metres.

YMOUSE − y co-ordinate of the mouse cursor, in pixels.

YPIXEL − height of a pixel in user co-ordinates.

YPLACE − y co-ordinate of the bottom left of a window on the visible screen, in pixels.

YPOS − y co-ordinate of the cursor in user co-ordinates.

YSCROLL − y co-ordinate of the bottom left of the window in the virtual screen, in user co-ordinates.

YUSABLE − height of the available screen, in pixels.

YVIRTUAL − height of the screen in user co-ordinates.

YWINDOW − height of a window in pixels.

Version 1.23 New Commands

Locomotive Software have a policy of continually upgrading Basic2, and are always willing to supply a disk containing the latest version for a modest sum. At the time of writing, the current upgrade is Version 1.23.

var=ALERT icon-num TEXT string(s) BUTTON string(2) throws an **ALERT** (selection) box onto the screen, containing up to three BUTTON boxes and a maximum of five lines of text. The icon number can be 0 = no icon, 1 = pointing hand, 2 = query, or 3 = Stop hand. The user can then select from the box by clicking on a button icon; and the variable **var** will return the number of the button. (Note that if you precede one of the BUTTON strings with **RETURN** it will be highlighted, and will be selected if the RETURN key is pressed.) As you can have no more than three buttons, the ALERT box is of limited value for menus, but it is handy for OOPS windows or YES/NO responses. For example, **choice=ALERT 3 TEXT "File has not", "been saved.", "Exit?" BUTTON "Yes" RETURN "No"**.

var=SELECTOR pathstring filespec provides a simple and effective means of accessing disk files. The command produces a screen box, identical to that called up by the Basic2 Load and Save routines. **pathstring** sets up the initial path, and may be omitted; **filespec** sets up the initial file specification. Wildcards may be used here, just as in the normal loading box. The variable **var** will return −1 if no file has been selected; otherwise 0. Three system variables are associated with this command: **selpath$** returns the path specification; **selfile$** returns the selected file; **selwild$** gives the wildcard specification, if used. For example, **fchoice=SELECTOR "B:/PROGS/" "*.APP"**.

INKEY$** has been modified slightly, so that it can get a character from the function and cursor keys − provided that the **OPTION INKEY$ command has been invoked. This creates a string of characters that can be associated with those non-printing keys.